# JavaScript: The Good Parts

## Other resources from O'Reilly

| | |
|---|---|
| **Related titles** | High Performance Web Sites     JavaScript: The Definitive |
| | JavaScript and DHTML     Guide |
| | Cookbook™     Learning JavaScript |

**oreilly.com**  *oreilly.com* is more than a complete catalog of O'Reilly books. You'll also find links to news, events, articles, weblogs, sample chapters, and code examples.

*oreillynet.com* is the essential portal for developers interested in open and emerging technologies, including new platforms, programming languages, and operating systems.

**Conferences**  O'Reilly brings diverse innovators together to nurture the ideas that spark revolutionary industries. We specialize in documenting the latest tools and systems, translating the innovator's knowledge into useful skills for those in the trenches. Visit *conferences.oreilly.com* for our upcoming events.

Safari Bookshelf (*safari.oreilly.com*) is the premier online reference library for programmers and IT professionals. Conduct searches across more than 1,000 books. Subscribers can zero in on answers to time-critical questions in a matter of seconds. Read the books on your Bookshelf from cover to cover or simply flip to the page you need. Try it today for free.

# JavaScript: The Good Parts

*Douglas Crockford*

**O'REILLY®**

Beijing · Cambridge · Farnham · Köln · Sebastopol · Tokyo

**JavaScript: The Good Parts**
by Douglas Crockford

Copyright © 2008 Yahoo! Inc. All rights reserved.
Printed in the United States of America.

Published by O'Reilly Media, Inc., 1005 Gravenstein Highway North, Sebastopol, CA 95472.

O'Reilly books may be purchased for educational, business, or sales promotional use. Online editions are also available for most titles (*safari.oreilly.com*). For more information, contact our corporate/institutional sales department: (800) 998-9938 or *corporate@oreilly.com*.

| | |
|---|---|
| **Editor:** Simon St.Laurent | **Indexer:** Julie Hawks |
| **Production Editor:** Sumita Mukherji | **Cover Designer:** Karen Montgomery |
| **Copyeditor:** Genevieve d'Entremont | **Interior Designer:** David Futato |
| **Proofreader:** Sumita Mukherji | **Illustrator:** Robert Romano |

**Printing History:**

|            |                |
|------------|----------------|
| May 2008:  | First Edition. |

ISBN: 978-0-596-51774-8
[LSI]                                                                      [2011-04-08]

*For the Lads: Clement, Philbert, Seymore, Stern,*
*and, lest we forget, C. Twildo.*

# Table of Contents

# Preface

> *If we offend, it is with our good will*
> *That you should think, we come not to offend,*
> *But with good will. To show our simple skill,*
> *That is the true beginning of our end.*
> —William Shakespeare, *A Midsummer Night's Dream*

This is a book about the JavaScript programming language. It is intended for programmers who, by happenstance or curiosity, are venturing into JavaScript for the first time. It is also intended for programmers who have been working with JavaScript at a novice level and are now ready for a more sophisticated relationship with the language. JavaScript is a surprisingly powerful language. Its unconventionality presents some challenges, but being a small language, it is easily mastered.

My goal here is to help you to learn to think in JavaScript. I will show you the components of the language and start you on the process of discovering the ways those components can be put together. This is not a reference book. It is not exhaustive about the language and its quirks. It doesn't contain everything you'll ever need to know. That stuff you can easily find online. Instead, this book just contains the things that are really important.

This is not a book for beginners. Someday I hope to write a *JavaScript: The First Parts* book, but this is not that book. This is not a book about Ajax or web programming. The focus is exclusively on JavaScript, which is just one of the languages the web developer must master.

This is not a book for dummies. This book is small, but it is dense. There is a lot of material packed into it. Don't be discouraged if it takes multiple readings to get it. Your efforts will be rewarded.

# Conventions Used in This Book

The following typographical conventions are used in this book:

*Italic*

> Indicates new terms, URLs, filenames, and file extensions.

`Constant width`

> Indicates computer coding in a broad sense. This includes commands, options, variables, attributes, keys, requests, functions, methods, types, classes, modules, properties, parameters, values, objects, events, event handlers, XML and XHTML tags, macros, and keywords.

**`Constant width bold`**

> Indicates commands or other text that should be typed literally by the user.

# Using Code Examples

This book is here to help you get your job done. In general, you may use the code in this book in your programs and documentation. You do not need to contact us for permission. For example, writing a program that uses several chunks of code from this book does not require permission. Selling or distributing a CD-ROM of examples from O'Reilly books does require permission. Answering a question by citing this book and quoting example code does not require permission. Incorporating a significant amount of example code from this book into your product's documentation does require permission.

We appreciate, but do not require, attribution. An attribution usually includes the title, author, publisher, and ISBN. For example: "*JavaScript: The Good Parts* by Douglas Crockford. Copyright 2008 Yahoo! Inc., 978-0-596-51774-8."

If you feel your use of code examples falls outside fair use or the permission given here, feel free to contact us at *permissions@oreilly.com*.

# Safari® Books Online

 When you see a Safari® Books Online icon on the cover of your favorite technology book, that means the book is available online through the O'Reilly Network Safari Bookshelf.

Safari offers a solution that's better than e-books. It's a virtual library that lets you easily search thousands of top tech books, cut and paste code samples, download chapters, and find quick answers when you need the most accurate, current information. Try it for free at *http://safari.oreilly.com*.

# How to Contact Us

Please address comments and questions concerning this book to the publisher:

O'Reilly Media, Inc.
1005 Gravenstein Highway North
Sebastopol, CA 95472
800-998-9938 (in the United States or Canada)
707-829-0515 (international or local)
707-829-0104 (fax)

We have a web page for this book, where we list errata, examples, and any additional information. You can access this page at:

*http://www.oreilly.com/catalog/9780596517748/*

To comment or ask technical questions about this book, send email to:

*bookquestions@oreilly.com*

For more information about our books, conferences, Resource Centers, and the O'Reilly Network, see our web site at:

*http://www.oreilly.com/*

# Acknowledgments

I want to thank the reviewers who pointed out my many egregious errors. There are few things better in life than having really smart people point out your blunders. It is even better when they do it before you go public. Thank you, Steve Souders, Bill Scott, Julien Lecomte, Stoyan Stefanov, Eric Miraglia, and Elliotte Rusty Harold.

I want to thank the people I worked with at Electric Communities and State Software who helped me discover that deep down there was goodness in this language, especially Chip Morningstar, Randy Farmer, John La, Mark Miller, Scott Shattuck, and Bill Edney.

I want to thank Yahoo! Inc. for giving me time to work on this project and for being such a great place to work, and thanks to all members of the Ajax Strike Force, past and present. I also want to thank O'Reilly Media, Inc., particularly Mary Treseler, Simon St.Laurent, and Sumita Mukherji for making things go so smoothly.

Special thanks to Professor Lisa Drake for all those things she does. And I want to thank the guys in ECMA TC39 who are struggling to make ECMAScript a better language.

Finally, thanks to Brendan Eich, the world's most misunderstood programming language designer, without whom this book would not have been necessary.

# CHAPTER 1

# Good Parts

*...setting the attractions of my*
*good parts aside I have no other charms.*
—William Shakespeare, *The Merry Wives of Windsor*

When I was a young journeyman programmer, I would learn about every feature of the languages I was using, and I would attempt to use all of those features when I wrote. I suppose it was a way of showing off, and I suppose it worked because I was the guy you went to if you wanted to know how to use a particular feature.

Eventually I figured out that some of those features were more trouble than they were worth. Some of them were poorly specified, and so were more likely to cause portability problems. Some resulted in code that was difficult to read or modify. Some induced me to write in a manner that was too tricky and error-prone. And some of those features were design errors. Sometimes language designers make mistakes.

Most programming languages contain good parts and bad parts. I discovered that I could be a better programmer by using only the good parts and avoiding the bad parts. After all, how can you build something good out of bad parts?

It is rarely possible for standards committees to remove imperfections from a language because doing so would cause the breakage of all of the bad programs that depend on those bad parts. They are usually powerless to do anything except heap more features on top of the existing pile of imperfections. And the new features do not always interact harmoniously, thus producing more bad parts.

But *you* have the power to define your own subset. You can write better programs by relying exclusively on the good parts.

JavaScript is a language with more than its share of bad parts. It went from nonexistence to global adoption in an alarmingly short period of time. It never had an interval in the lab when it could be tried out and polished. It went straight into Netscape Navigator 2 just as it was, and it was very rough. When Java™ applets failed, JavaScript became the "Language of the Web" by default. JavaScript's popularity is almost completely independent of its qualities as a programming language.

Fortunately, JavaScript has some extraordinarily good parts. In JavaScript, there is a beautiful, elegant, highly expressive language that is buried under a steaming pile of good intentions and blunders. The best nature of JavaScript is so effectively hidden that for many years the prevailing opinion of JavaScript was that it was an unsightly, incompetent toy. My intention here is to expose the goodness in JavaScript, an outstanding, dynamic programming language. JavaScript is a block of marble, and I chip away the features that are not beautiful until the language's true nature reveals itself. I believe that the elegant subset I carved out is vastly superior to the language as a whole, being more reliable, readable, and maintainable.

This book will not attempt to fully describe the language. Instead, it will focus on the good parts with occasional warnings to avoid the bad. The subset that will be described here can be used to construct reliable, readable programs small and large. By focusing on just the good parts, we can reduce learning time, increase robustness, and save some trees.

Perhaps the greatest benefit of studying the good parts is that you can avoid the need to unlearn the bad parts. Unlearning bad patterns is very difficult. It is a painful task that most of us face with extreme reluctance. Sometimes languages are subsetted to make them work better for students. But in this case, I am subsetting JavaScript to make it work better for professionals.

# Why JavaScript?

JavaScript is an important language because it is the language of the web browser. Its association with the browser makes it one of the most popular programming languages in the world. At the same time, it is one of the most despised programming languages in the world. The API of the browser, the Document Object Model (DOM) is quite awful, and JavaScript is unfairly blamed. The DOM would be painful to work with in any language. The DOM is poorly specified and inconsistently implemented. This book touches only very lightly on the DOM. I think writing a *Good Parts* book about the DOM would be extremely challenging.

JavaScript is most despised because it isn't SOME OTHER LANGUAGE. If you are good in SOME OTHER LANGUAGE and you have to program in an environment that only supports JavaScript, then you are forced to use JavaScript, and that is annoying. Most people in that situation don't even bother to learn JavaScript first, and then they are surprised when JavaScript turns out to have significant differences from the SOME OTHER LANGUAGE they would rather be using, and that those differences matter.

The amazing thing about JavaScript is that it is possible to get work done with it without knowing much about the language, or even knowing much about programming. It is a language with enormous expressive power. It is even better when you know what you're doing. Programming is difficult business. It should never be undertaken in ignorance.

# Analyzing JavaScript

JavaScript is built on some very good ideas and a few very bad ones.

The very good ideas include functions, loose typing, dynamic objects, and an expressive object literal notation. The bad ideas include a programming model based on global variables.

JavaScript's functions are first class objects with (mostly) lexical scoping. JavaScript is the first lambda language to go mainstream. Deep down, JavaScript has more in common with Lisp and Scheme than with Java. It is Lisp in C's clothing. This makes JavaScript a remarkably powerful language.

The fashion in most programming languages today demands strong typing. The theory is that strong typing allows a compiler to detect a large class of errors at compile time. The sooner we can detect and repair errors, the less they cost us. JavaScript is a loosely typed language, so JavaScript compilers are unable to detect type errors. This can be alarming to people who are coming to JavaScript from strongly typed languages. But it turns out that strong typing does not eliminate the need for careful testing. And I have found in my work that the sorts of errors that strong type checking finds are not the errors I worry about. On the other hand, I find loose typing to be liberating. I don't need to form complex class hierarchies. And I never have to cast or wrestle with the type system to get the behavior that I want.

JavaScript has a very powerful object literal notation. Objects can be created simply by listing their components. This notation was the inspiration for JSON, the popular data interchange format. (There will be more about JSON in Appendix E.)

A controversial feature in JavaScript is prototypal inheritance. JavaScript has a class-free object system in which objects inherit properties directly from other objects. This is really powerful, but it is unfamiliar to classically trained programmers. If you attempt to apply classical design patterns directly to JavaScript, you will be frustrated. But if you learn to work with JavaScript's prototypal nature, your efforts will be rewarded.

JavaScript is much maligned for its choice of key ideas. For the most part, though, those choices were good, if unusual. But there was one choice that was particularly bad: JavaScript depends on global variables for linkage. All of the top-level variables of all compilation units are tossed together in a common namespace called *the global object*. This is a bad thing because global variables are evil, and in JavaScript they are fundamental. Fortunately, as we will see, JavaScript also gives us the tools to mitigate this problem.

In a few cases, we can't ignore the bad parts. There are some unavoidable awful parts, which will be called out as they occur. They will also be summarized in Appendix A. But we will succeed in avoiding most of the bad parts in this book, summarizing much of what was left out in Appendix B. If you want to learn more about the bad parts and how to use them badly, consult any other JavaScript book.

The standard that defines JavaScript (aka JScript) is the third edition of *The ECMAScript Programming Language*, which is available from *http://www.ecma-international.org/publications/files/ecma-st/ECMA-262.pdf*. The language described in this book is a proper subset of ECMAScript. This book does not describe the whole language because it leaves out the bad parts. The treatment here is not exhaustive. It avoids the edge cases. You should, too. There is danger and misery at the edges.

Appendix C describes a programming tool called JSLint, a JavaScript parser that can analyze a JavaScript program and report on the bad parts that it contains. JSLint provides a degree of rigor that is generally lacking in JavaScript development. It can give you confidence that your programs contain only the good parts.

JavaScript is a language of many contrasts. It contains many errors and sharp edges, so you might wonder, "Why should I use JavaScript?" There are two answers. The first is that you don't have a choice. The Web has become an important platform for application development, and JavaScript is the only language that is found in all browsers. It is unfortunate that Java failed in that environment; if it hadn't, there could be a choice for people desiring a strongly typed classical language. But Java did fail and JavaScript is flourishing, so there is evidence that JavaScript did something right.

The other answer is that, despite its deficiencies, *JavaScript is really good*. It is lightweight and expressive. And once you get the hang of it, functional programming is a lot of fun.

But in order to use the language well, you must be well informed about its limitations. I will pound on those with some brutality. Don't let that discourage you. The good parts are good enough to compensate for the bad parts.

# A Simple Testing Ground

If you have a web browser and any text editor, you have everything you need to run JavaScript programs. First, make an HTML file with a name like *program.html*:

```
<html><body><pre><script src="program.js">
</script></pre></body></html>
```

Then, make a file in the same directory with a name like *program.js*:

```
document.writeln('Hello, world!');
```

Next, open your HTML file in your browser to see the result. Throughout the book, a method method is used to define new methods. This is its definition:

```
Function.prototype.method = function (name, func) {
    this.prototype[name] = func;
    return this;
};
```

It will be explained in Chapter 4.

# CHAPTER 2

# Grammar

*I know it well:*
*I read it in the grammar long ago.*
—William Shakespeare, *The Tragedy of Titus Andronicus*

This chapter introduces the grammar of the good parts of JavaScript, presenting a quick overview of how the language is structured. We will represent the grammar with railroad diagrams.

The rules for interpreting these diagrams are simple:

- You start on the left edge and follow the tracks to the right edge.
- As you go, you will encounter literals in ovals, and rules or descriptions in rectangles.
- Any sequence that can be made by following the tracks is legal.
- Any sequence that cannot be made by following the tracks is not legal.
- Railroad diagrams with one bar at each end allow whitespace to be inserted between any pair of tokens. Railroad diagrams with two bars at each end do not.

The grammar of the good parts presented in this chapter is significantly simpler than the grammar of the whole language.

## Whitespace

Whitespace can take the form of formatting characters or comments. Whitespace is usually insignificant, but it is occasionally necessary to use whitespace to separate sequences of characters that would otherwise be combined into a single token. For example, in:

```
var that = this;
```

the space between var and that cannot be removed, but the other spaces can be removed.

*whitespace*

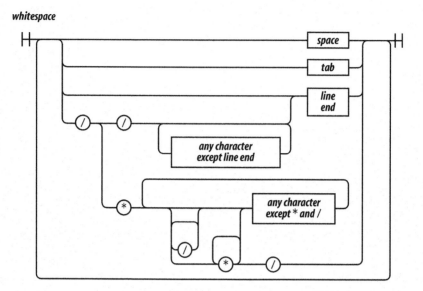

JavaScript offers two forms of comments, block comments formed with /* */ and line-ending comments starting with //. Comments should be used liberally to improve the readability of your programs. Take care that the comments always accurately describe the code. Obsolete comments are worse than no comments.

The /* */ form of block comments came from a language called PL/I. PL/I chose those strange pairs as the symbols for comments because they were unlikely to occur in that language's programs, except perhaps in string literals. In JavaScript, those pairs can also occur in regular expression literals, so block comments are not safe for commenting out blocks of code. For example:

```
/*
    var rm_a = /a*/.match(s);
*/
```

causes a syntax error. So, it is recommended that /* */ comments be avoided and // comments be used instead. In this book, // will be used exclusively.

# Names

A name is a letter optionally followed by one or more letters, digits, or underbars. A name cannot be one of these reserved words:

```
abstract
boolean break byte
case catch char class const continue
debugger default delete do double
```

```
else enum export extends
false final finally float for function
goto
if implements import in instanceof int interface
long
native new null
package private protected public
return
short static super switch synchronized
this throw throws transient true try typeof
var volatile void
while with
```

*name*

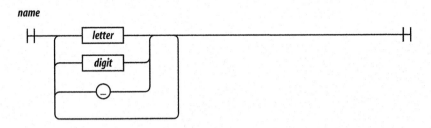

Most of the reserved words in this list are not used in the language. The list does not include some words that should have been reserved but were not, such as undefined, NaN, and Infinity. It is not permitted to name a variable or parameter with a reserved word. Worse, it is not permitted to use a reserved word as the name of an object property in an object literal or following a dot in a refinement.

Names are used for statements, variables, parameters, property names, operators, and labels.

# Numbers

*number literal*

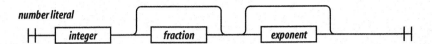

JavaScript has a single number type. Internally, it is represented as 64-bit floating point, the same as Java's double. Unlike most other programming languages, there is no separate integer type, so 1 and 1.0 are the same value. This is a significant convenience because problems of overflow in short integers are completely avoided, and all you need to know about a number is that it is a number. A large class of numeric type errors is avoided.

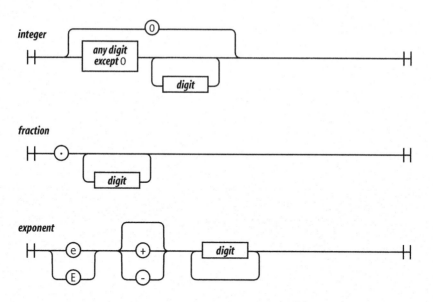

If a number literal has an exponent part, then the value of the literal is computed by multiplying the part before the e by 10 raised to the power of the part after the e. So 100 and 1e2 are the same number.

Negative numbers can be formed by using the – prefix operator.

The value NaN is a number value that is the result of an operation that cannot produce a normal result. NaN is not equal to any value, including itself. You can detect NaN with the isNaN(*number*) function.

The value Infinity represents all values greater than 1.79769313486231570e+308.

Numbers have methods (see Chapter 8). JavaScript has a Math object that contains a set of methods that act on numbers. For example, the Math.floor(*number*) method can be used to convert a number into an integer.

# Strings

A string literal can be wrapped in single quotes or double quotes. It can contain zero or more characters. The \ (backslash) is the escape character. JavaScript was built at a time when Unicode was a 16-bit character set, so all characters in JavaScript are 16 bits wide.

JavaScript does not have a character type. To represent a character, make a string with just one character in it.

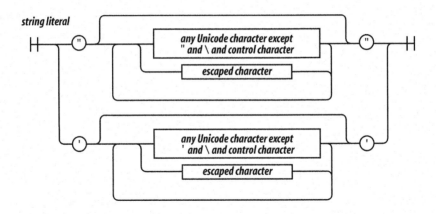

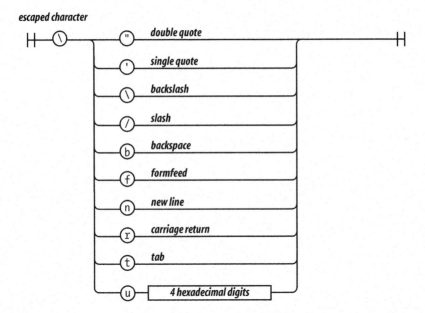

The escape sequences allow for inserting characters into strings that are not normally permitted, such as backslashes, quotes, and control characters. The \u convention allows for specifying character code points numerically.

```
"A" === "\u0041"
```

Strings have a length property. For example, "seven".length is 5.

Strings are immutable. Once it is made, a string can never be changed. But it is easy to make a new string by concatenating other strings together with the + operator.

Two strings containing exactly the same characters in the same order are considered to be the same string. So:

```
'c' + 'a' + 't' === 'cat'
```

is true.

Strings have methods (see Chapter 8):

```
'cat'.toUpperCase( ) === 'CAT'
```

# Statements

*var statements*

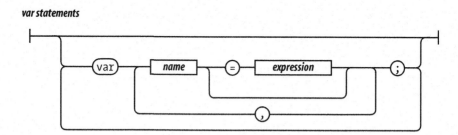

A compilation unit contains a set of executable statements. In web browsers, each `<script>` tag delivers a compilation unit that is compiled and immediately executed. Lacking a linker, JavaScript throws them all together in a common global namespace. There is more on global variables in Appendix A.

When used inside of a function, the `var` statement defines the function's private variables.

The `switch`, `while`, `for`, and `do` statements are allowed to have an optional *label* prefix that interacts with the `break` statement.

Statements tend to be executed in order from top to bottom. The sequence of execution can be altered by the conditional statements (`if` and `switch`), by the looping statements (`while`, `for`, and `do`), by the disruptive statements (`break`, `return`, and `throw`), and by function invocation.

A block is a set of statements wrapped in curly braces. Unlike many other languages, blocks in JavaScript do not create a new scope, so variables should be defined at the top of the function, not in blocks.

The `if` statement changes the flow of the program based on the value of the expression. The *then* block is executed if the expression is *truthy*; otherwise, the optional `else` branch is taken.

**statements**

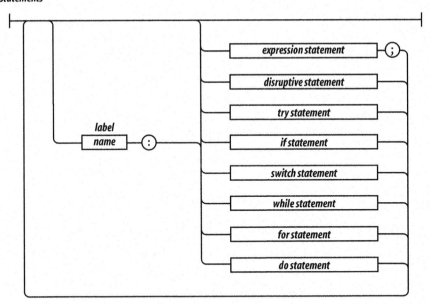

**disruptive statement**

**block**

**if statement**

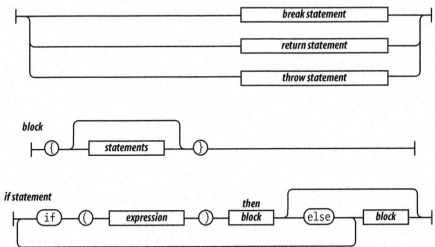

Here are the *falsy* values:

- false
- null

- undefined
- The empty string `''`
- The number 0
- The number NaN

All other values are truthy, including true, the string `'false'`, and all objects.

**switch statement**

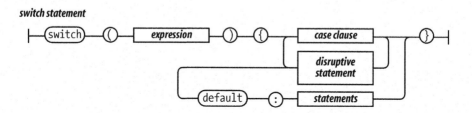

The switch statement performs a multiway branch. It compares the expression for equality with all of the specified cases. The expression can produce a number or a string. When an exact match is found, the statements of the matching case clause are executed. If there is no match, the optional default statements are executed.

**case clause**

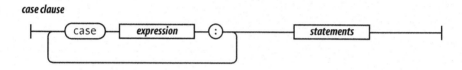

A case clause contains one or more case expressions. The case expressions need not be constants. The statement following a clause should be a disruptive statement to prevent fall through into the next case. The break statement can be used to exit from a switch.

**while statement**

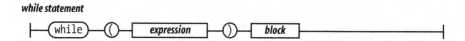

The while statement performs a simple loop. If the expression is falsy, then the loop will break. While the expression is truthy, the block will be executed.

The for statement is a more complicated looping statement. It comes in two forms.

The conventional form is controlled by three optional clauses: the *initialization*, the *condition*, and the *increment*. First, the initialization is done, which typically initializes the loop variable. Then, the *condition* is evaluated. Typically, this tests the loop variable against a completion criterion. If the *condition* is omitted, then a *condition* of true is assumed. If the *condition* is falsy, the loop breaks. Otherwise, the block is executed, then the *increment* executes, and then the loop repeats with the *condition*.

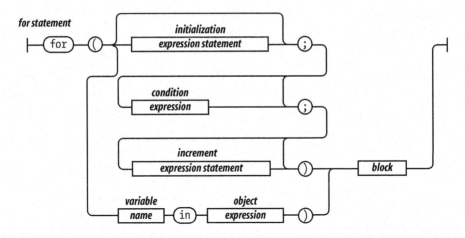

*for statement*

The other form (called for in) enumerates the property names (or keys) of an object. On each iteration, another property name string from the *object* is assigned to the *variable*.

It is usually necessary to test *object*.hasOwnProperty(*variable*) to determine whether the property name is truly a member of the object or was found instead on the prototype chain.

```
for (myvar in obj) {
    if (obj.hasOwnProperty(myvar)) {
        ...
    }
}
```

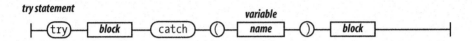

*do statement*

The do statement is like the while statement except that the expression is tested after the block is executed instead of before. That means that the block will always be executed at least once.

*try statement*

The try statement executes a block and catches any exceptions that were thrown by the block. The catch clause defines a new *variable* that will receive the exception object.

*throw statement*

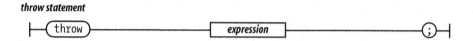

The throw statement raises an exception. If the throw statement is in a try block, then control goes to the catch clause. Otherwise, the function invocation is abandoned, and control goes to the catch clause of the try in the calling function.

The expression is usually an object literal containing a name property and a message property. The catcher of the exception can use that information to determine what to do.

*return statement*

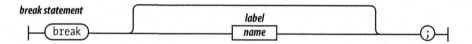

The return statement causes the early return from a function. It can also specify the value to be returned. If a return expression is not specified, then the return value will be undefined.

JavaScript does not allow a line end between the return and the expression.

*break statement*

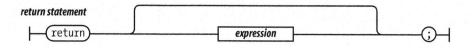

The break statement causes the exit from a loop statement or a switch statement. It can optionally have a *label* that will cause an exit from the labeled statement.

JavaScript does not allow a line end between the break and the label.

*expression statement*

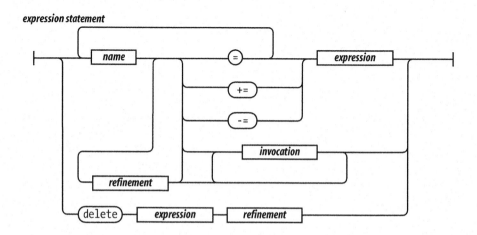

An expression statement can either assign values to one or more variables or members, invoke a method, delete a property from an object. The = operator is used for assignment. Do not confuse it with the === equality operator. The += operator can add or concatenate.

# Expressions

*expression*

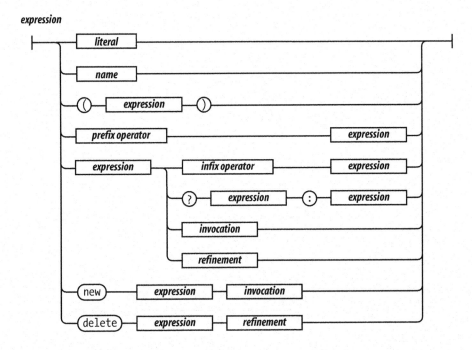

The simplest expressions are a literal value (such as a string or number), a variable, a built-in value (true, false, null, undefined, NaN, or Infinity), an invocation expression preceded by new, a refinement expression preceded by delete, an expression wrapped in parentheses, an expression preceded by a prefix operator, or an expression followed by:

- An infix operator and another expression
- The ? ternary operator followed by another expression, then by :, and then by yet another expression
- An invocation
- A refinement

The ? ternary operator takes three operands. If the first operand is truthy, it produces the value of the second operand. But if the first operand is falsy, it produces the value of the third operand.

The operators at the top of the operator precedence list in Table 2-1 have higher precedence. They bind the tightest. The operators at the bottom have the lowest precedence. Parentheses can be used to alter the normal precedence, so:

```
2 + 3 * 5 === 17
(2 + 3) * 5 === 25
```

*Table 2-1. Operator precedence*

| | |
|---|---|
| . [] () | Refinement and invocation |
| delete new typeof + - ! | Unary operators |
| * / % | Multiplication, division, remainder |
| + - | Addition/concatenation, subtraction |
| >= <= > < | Inequality |
| === !== | Equality |
| && | Logical and |
| \|\| | Logical or |
| ?: | Ternary |

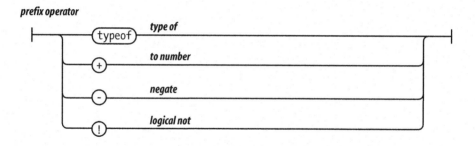

The values produced by typeof are 'number', 'string', 'boolean', 'undefined', 'function', and 'object'. If the operand is an array or null, then the result is 'object', which is wrong. There will be more about typeof in Chapter 6 and Appendix A.

If the operand of ! is truthy, it produces false. Otherwise, it produces true.

The + operator adds or concatenates. If you want it to add, make sure both operands are numbers.

The / operator can produce a noninteger result even if both operands are integers.

The && operator produces the value of its first operand if the first operand is falsy. Otherwise, it produces the value of the second operand.

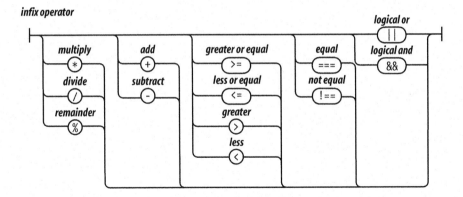

*infix operator*

The || operator produces the value of its first operand if the first operand is truthy. Otherwise, it produces the value of the second operand.

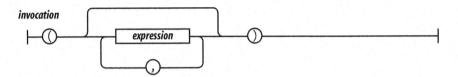

*invocation*

Invocation causes the execution of a function value. The invocation operator is a pair of parentheses that follow the function value. The parentheses can contain arguments that will be delivered to the function. There will be much more about functions in Chapter 4.

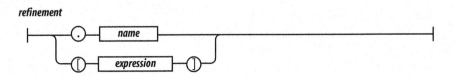

*refinement*

A refinement is used to specify a property or element of an object or array. This will be described in detail in the next chapter.

## Literals

Object literals are a convenient notation for specifying new objects. The names of the properties can be specified as names or as strings. The names are treated as literal names, not as variable names, so the names of the properties of the object must be known at compile time. The values of the properties are expressions. There will be more about object literals in the next chapter.

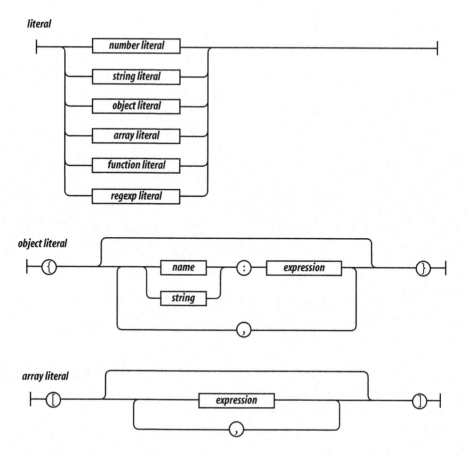

Array literals are a convenient notation for specifying new arrays. There will be more about array literals in Chapter 6.

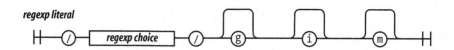

There will be more about regular expressions in Chapter 7.

# Functions

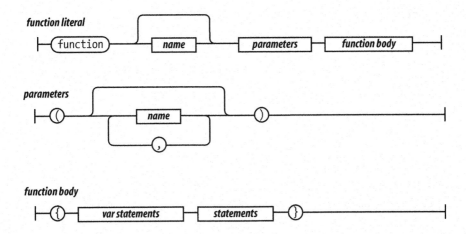

A function literal defines a function value. It can have an optional name that it can use to call itself recursively. It can specify a list of parameters that will act as variables initialized by the invocation arguments. The body of the function includes variable definitions and statements. There will be more about functions in Chapter 4.

# CHAPTER 3

# Objects

*Upon a homely object Love can wink.*
—William Shakespeare, *The Two Gentlemen of Verona*

The simple types of JavaScript are numbers, strings, booleans (true and false), null, and undefined. All other values are *objects*. Numbers, strings, and booleans are object-like in that they have methods, but they are immutable. Objects in JavaScript are mutable keyed collections. In JavaScript, arrays are objects, functions are objects, regular expressions are objects, and, of course, objects are objects.

An object is a container of properties, where a property has a name and a value. A property name can be any string, including the empty string. A property value can be any JavaScript value except for undefined.

Objects in JavaScript are class-free. There is no constraint on the names of new properties or on the values of properties. Objects are useful for collecting and organizing data. Objects can contain other objects, so they can easily represent tree or graph structures.

JavaScript includes a prototype linkage feature that allows one object to inherit the properties of another. When used well, this can reduce object initialization time and memory consumption.

## Object Literals

Object literals provide a very convenient notation for creating new object values. An object literal is a pair of curly braces surrounding zero or more name/value pairs. An object literal can appear anywhere an expression can appear:

```
var empty_object = {};

var stooge = {
    "first-name": "Jerome",
    "last-name": "Howard"
};
```

A property's name can be any string, including the empty string. The quotes around a property's name in an object literal are optional if the name would be a legal JavaScript name and not a reserved word. So quotes are required around "first-name", but are optional around first_name. Commas are used to separate the pairs.

A property's value can be obtained from any expression, including another object literal. Objects can nest:

```
var flight = {
    airline: "Oceanic",
    number: 815,
    departure: {
        IATA: "SYD",
        time: "2004-09-22 14:55",
        city: "Sydney"
    },
    arrival: {
        IATA: "LAX",
        time: "2004-09-23 10:42",
        city: "Los Angeles"
    }
};
```

# Retrieval

Values can be retrieved from an object by wrapping a string expression in a [ ] suffix. If the string expression is a string literal, and if it is a legal JavaScript name and not a reserved word, then the . notation can be used instead. The . notation is preferred because it is more compact and it reads better:

```
stooge["first-name"]      // "Jerome"
flight.departure.IATA     // "SYD"
```

The undefined value is produced if an attempt is made to retrieve a nonexistent member:

```
stooge["middle-name"]     // undefined
flight.status             // undefined
stooge["FIRST-NAME"]      // undefined
```

The || operator can be used to fill in default values:

```
var middle = stooge["middle-name"] || "(none)";
var status = flight.status || "unknown";
```

Attempting to retrieve values from undefined will throw a TypeError exception. This can be guarded against with the && operator:

```
flight.equipment                              // undefined
flight.equipment.model                        // throw "TypeError"
flight.equipment && flight.equipment.model    // undefined
```

# Update

A value in an object can be updated by assignment. If the property name already exists in the object, the property value is replaced:

```
stooge['first-name'] = 'Jerome';
```

If the object does not already have that property name, the object is augmented:

```
stooge['middle-name'] = 'Lester';
stooge.nickname = 'Curly';
flight.equipment = {
    model: 'Boeing 777'
};
flight.status = 'overdue';
```

# Reference

Objects are passed around by reference. They are never copied:

```
var x = stooge;
x.nickname = 'Curly';
var nick = stooge.nickname;
    // nick is 'Curly' because x and stooge
    // are references to the same object

var a = {}, b = {}, c = {};
    // a, b, and c each refer to a
    // different empty object
a = b = c = {};
    // a, b, and c all refer to
    // the same empty object
```

# Prototype

Every object is linked to a prototype object from which it can inherit properties. All objects created from object literals are linked to Object.prototype, an object that comes standard with JavaScript.

When you make a new object, you can select the object that should be its prototype. The mechanism that JavaScript provides to do this is messy and complex, but it can be significantly simplified. We will add a create method to the Object function. The create method creates a new object that uses an old object as its prototype. There will be much more about functions in the next chapter.

```
if (typeof Object.create !== 'function') {
    Object.create = function (o) {
        var F = function () {};
        F.prototype = o;
        return new F();
    };
```

---

```
        }
        var another_stooge = Object.create(stooge);
```

The prototype link has no effect on updating. When we make changes to an object, the object's prototype is not touched:

```
        another_stooge['first-name'] = 'Harry';
        another_stooge['middle-name'] = 'Moses';
        another_stooge.nickname = 'Moe';
```

The prototype link is used only in retrieval. If we try to retrieve a property value from an object, and if the object lacks the property name, then JavaScript attempts to retrieve the property value from the prototype object. And if that object is lacking the property, then it goes to *its* prototype, and so on until the process finally bottoms out with Object.prototype. If the desired property exists nowhere in the prototype chain, then the result is the undefined value. This is called *delegation*.

The prototype relationship is a dynamic relationship. If we add a new property to a prototype, that property will immediately be visible in all of the objects that are based on that prototype:

```
        stooge.profession = 'actor';
        another_stooge.profession    // 'actor'
```

We will see more about the prototype chain in Chapter 6.

# Reflection

It is easy to inspect an object to determine what properties it has by attempting to retrieve the properties and examining the values obtained. The typeof operator can be very helpful in determining the type of a property:

```
        typeof flight.number    // 'number'
        typeof flight.status    // 'string'
        typeof flight.arrival   // 'object'
        typeof flight.manifest  // 'undefined'
```

Some care must be taken because any property on the prototype chain can produce a value:

```
        typeof flight.toString    // 'function'
        typeof flight.constructor // 'function'
```

There are two approaches to dealing with these undesired properties. The first is to have your program look for and reject function values. Generally, when you are reflecting, you are interested in data, and so you should be aware that some values could be functions.

The other approach is to use the hasOwnProperty method, which returns true if the object has a particular property. The hasOwnProperty method does not look at the prototype chain:

```
        flight.hasOwnProperty('number')        // true
        flight.hasOwnProperty('constructor')   // false
```

# Enumeration

The `for in` statement can loop over all of the property names in an object. The enumeration will include all of the properties—including functions and prototype properties that you might not be interested in—so it is necessary to filter out the values you don't want. The most common filters are the `hasOwnProperty` method and using `typeof` to exclude functions:

```
var name;
for (name in another_stooge) {
    if (typeof another_stooge[name] !== 'function') {
        document.writeln(name + ': ' + another_stooge[name]);
    }
}
```

There is no guarantee on the order of the names, so be prepared for the names to appear in any order. If you want to assure that the properties appear in a particular order, it is best to avoid the `for in` statement entirely and instead make an array containing the names of the properties in the correct order:

```
var i;
var properties = [
    'first-name',
    'middle-name',
    'last-name',
    'profession'
];
for (i = 0; i < properties.length; i += 1) {
    document.writeln(properties[i] + ': ' +
            another_stooge[properties[i]]);
}
```

By using `for` instead of `for in`, we were able to get the properties we wanted without worrying about what might be dredged up from the prototype chain, and we got them in the correct order.

# Delete

The `delete` operator can be used to remove a property from an object. It will remove a property from the object if it has one. It will not touch any of the objects in the prototype linkage.

Removing a property from an object may allow a property from the prototype linkage to shine through:

```
another_stooge.nickname    // 'Moe'

// Remove nickname from another_stooge, revealing
// the nickname of the prototype.
```

```
delete another_stooge.nickname;

another_stooge.nickname    // 'Curly'
```

# Global Abatement

JavaScript makes it easy to define global variables that can hold all of the assets of your application. Unfortunately, global variables weaken the resiliency of programs and should be avoided.

One way to minimize the use of global variables is to create a single global variable for your application:

```
var MYAPP = {};
```

That variable then becomes the container for your application:

```
MYAPP.stooge = {
    "first-name": "Joe",
    "last-name": "Howard"
};

MYAPP.flight = {
    airline: "Oceanic",
    number: 815,
    departure: {
        IATA: "SYD",
        time: "2004-09-22 14:55",
        city: "Sydney"
    },
    arrival: {
        IATA: "LAX",
        time: "2004-09-23 10:42",
        city: "Los Angeles"
    }
};
```

By reducing your global footprint to a single name, you significantly reduce the chance of bad interactions with other applications, widgets, or libraries. Your program also becomes easier to read because it is obvious that MYAPP.stooge refers to a top-level structure. In the next chapter, we will see ways to use closure for information hiding, which is another effective global abatement technique.

# CHAPTER 4

# Functions

*Why, every fault's condemn'd ere it be done:*
*Mine were the very cipher of a function…*
—William Shakespeare, *Measure for Measure*

The best thing about JavaScript is its implementation of functions. It got almost everything right. But, as you should expect with JavaScript, it didn't get everything right.

A function encloses a set of statements. Functions are the fundamental modular unit of JavaScript. They are used for code reuse, information hiding, and composition. Functions are used to specify the behavior of objects. Generally, the craft of programming is the factoring of a set of requirements into a set of functions and data structures.

## Function Objects

Functions in JavaScript are objects. Objects are collections of name/value pairs having a hidden link to a prototype object. Objects produced from object literals are linked to `Object.prototype`. Function objects are linked to `Function.prototype` (which is itself linked to `Object.prototype`). Every function is also created with two additional hidden properties: the function's context and the code that implements the function's behavior.

Every function object is also created with a `prototype` property. Its value is an object with a `constructor` property whose value is the function. This is distinct from the hidden link to `Function.prototype`. The meaning of this convoluted construction will be revealed in the next chapter.

Since functions are objects, they can be used like any other value. Functions can be stored in variables, objects, and arrays. Functions can be passed as arguments to functions, and functions can be returned from functions. Also, since functions are objects, functions can have methods.

The thing that is special about functions is that they can be invoked.

# Function Literal

Function objects are created with function literals:

```
// Create a variable called add and store a function
// in it that adds two numbers.

var add = function (a, b) {
    return a + b;
};
```

A function literal has four parts. The first part is the reserved word `function`.

The optional second part is the function's name. The function can use its name to call itself recursively. The name can also be used by debuggers and development tools to identify the function. If a function is not given a name, as shown in the previous example, it is said to be *anonymous*.

The third part is the set of parameters of the function, wrapped in parentheses. Within the parentheses is a set of zero or more parameter names, separated by commas. These names will be defined as variables in the function. Unlike ordinary variables, instead of being initialized to `undefined`, they will be initialized to the arguments supplied when the function is invoked.

The fourth part is a set of statements wrapped in curly braces. These statements are the body of the function. They are executed when the function is invoked.

A function literal can appear anywhere that an expression can appear. Functions can be defined inside of other functions. An inner function of course has access to its parameters and variables. An inner function also enjoys access to the parameters and variables of the functions it is nested within. The function object created by a function literal contains a link to that outer context. This is called *closure*. This is the source of enormous expressive power.

# Invocation

Invoking a function suspends the execution of the current function, passing control and parameters to the new function. In addition to the declared parameters, every function receives two additional parameters: `this` and `arguments`. The `this` parameter is very important in object oriented programming, and its value is determined by the *invocation pattern*. There are four patterns of invocation in JavaScript: the method invocation pattern, the function invocation pattern, the constructor invocation pattern, and the apply invocation pattern. The patterns differ in how the bonus parameter `this` is initialized.

The invocation operator is a pair of parentheses that follow any expression that produces a function value. The parentheses can contain zero or more expressions, separated by commas. Each expression produces one argument value. Each of the argument values will be assigned to the function's parameter names. There is no runtime error when the number of arguments and the number of parameters do not match. If there are too many argument values, the extra argument values will be ignored. If there are too few argument values, the undefined value will be substituted for the missing values. There is no type checking on the argument values: any type of value can be passed to any parameter.

## The Method Invocation Pattern

When a function is stored as a property of an object, we call it a *method*. When a method is invoked, this is bound to that object. If an invocation expression contains a refinement (that is, a . dot expression or [*subscript*] expression), it is invoked as a method:

```
// Create myObject. It has a value and an increment
// method. The increment method takes an optional
// parameter. If the argument is not a number, then 1
// is used as the default.

var myObject = {
    value: 0,
    increment: function (inc) {
        this.value += typeof inc === 'number' ? inc : 1;
    }
};

myObject.increment( );
document.writeln(myObject.value);    // 1

myObject.increment(2);
document.writeln(myObject.value);    // 3
```

A method can use this to access the object so that it can retrieve values from the object or modify the object. The binding of this to the object happens at invocation time. This very late binding makes functions that use this highly reusable. Methods that get their object context from this are called *public methods*.

## The Function Invocation Pattern

When a function is not the property of an object, then it is invoked as a function:

```
var sum = add(3, 4);    // sum is 7
```

When a function is invoked with this pattern, this is bound to the global object. This was a mistake in the design of the language. Had the language been designed correctly, when the inner function is invoked, this would still be bound to the this variable of the outer function. A consequence of this error is that a method cannot employ an inner function to help it do its work because the inner function does not share the method's access to the object as its this is bound to the wrong value. Fortunately, there is an easy workaround. If the method defines a variable and assigns it the value of this, the inner function will have access to this through that variable. By convention, the name of that variable is that:

```
// Augment myObject with a double method.

myObject.double = function ( ) {
    var that = this;     // Workaround.

    var helper = function ( ) {
        that.value = add(that.value, that.value);
    };

    helper( );     // Invoke helper as a function.
};

// Invoke double as a method.

myObject.double( );
document.writeln(myObject.value);
```

## The Constructor Invocation Pattern

JavaScript is a *prototypal* inheritance language. That means that objects can inherit properties directly from other objects. The language is class-free.

This is a radical departure from the current fashion. Most languages today are *classical*. Prototypal inheritance is powerfully expressive, but is not widely understood. JavaScript itself is not confident in its prototypal nature, so it offers an object-making syntax that is reminiscent of the classical languages. Few classical programmers found prototypal inheritance to be acceptable, and classically inspired syntax obscures the language's true prototypal nature. It is the worst of both worlds.

If a function is invoked with the new prefix, then a new object will be created with a hidden link to the value of the function's prototype member, and this will be bound to that new object.

The new prefix also changes the behavior of the return statement. We will see more about that next.

```
// Create a constructor function called Quo.
// It makes an object with a status property.

var Quo = function (string) {
    this.status = string;
};

// Give all instances of Quo a public method
```

```
// called get_status.

Quo.prototype.get_status = function () {
    return this.status;
};

// Make an instance of Quo.

var myQuo = new Quo("confused");

document.writeln(myQuo.get_status()); // confused
```

Functions that are intended to be used with the new prefix are called *constructors*. By convention, they are kept in variables with a capitalized name. If a constructor is called without the new prefix, very bad things can happen without a compile-time or runtime warning, so the capitalization convention is really important.

Use of this style of constructor functions is not recommended. We will see better alternatives in the next chapter.

## The Apply Invocation Pattern

Because JavaScript is a functional object-oriented language, functions can have methods.

The apply method lets us construct an array of arguments to use to invoke a function. It also lets us choose the value of this. The apply method takes two parameters. The first is the value that should be bound to this. The second is an array of parameters.

```
// Make an array of 2 numbers and add them.

var array = [3, 4];
var sum = add.apply(null, array);    // sum is 7

// Make an object with a status member.

var statusObject = {
    status: 'A-OK'
};

// statusObject does not inherit from Quo.prototype,
// but we can invoke the get_status method on
// statusObject even though statusObject does not have
// a get_status method.

var status = Quo.prototype.get_status.apply(statusObject);
    // status is 'A-OK'
```

# Arguments

A bonus parameter that is available to functions when they are invoked is the arguments array. It gives the function access to all of the arguments that were supplied with the invocation, including excess arguments that were not assigned to parameters. This makes it possible to write functions that take an unspecified number of parameters:

```
// Make a function that adds a lot of stuff.

// Note that defining the variable sum inside of
// the function does not interfere with the sum
// defined outside of the function. The function
// only sees the inner one.

var sum = function () {
    var i, sum = 0;
    for (i = 0; i < arguments.length; i += 1) {
        sum += arguments[i];
    }
    return sum;
};

document.writeln(sum(4, 8, 15, 16, 23, 42)); // 108
```

This is not a particularly useful pattern. In Chapter 6, we will see how we can add a similar method to an array.

Because of a design error, arguments is not really an array. It is an array-like object. arguments has a length property, but it lacks all of the array methods. We will see a consequence of that design error at the end of this chapter.

# Return

When a function is invoked, it begins execution with the first statement, and ends when it hits the } that closes the function body. That causes the function to return control to the part of the program that invoked the function.

The return statement can be used to cause the function to return early. When return is executed, the function returns immediately without executing the remaining statements.

A function always returns a value. If the return value is not specified, then undefined is returned.

If the function was invoked with the new prefix and the return value is not an object, then this (the new object) is returned instead.

# Exceptions

JavaScript provides an exception handling mechanism. Exceptions are unusual (but not completely unexpected) mishaps that interfere with the normal flow of a program. When such a mishap is detected, your program should throw an exception:

```
var add = function (a, b) {
    if (typeof a !== 'number' || typeof b !== 'number') {
        throw {
            name: 'TypeError',
            message: 'add needs numbers'
        };
    }
    return a + b;
}
```

The `throw` statement interrupts execution of the function. It should be given an exception object containing a `name` property that identifies the type of the exception, and a descriptive `message` property. You can also add other properties.

The exception object will be delivered to the `catch` clause of a `try` statement:

```
// Make a try_it function that calls the new add
// function incorrectly.

var try_it = function () {
    try {
        add("seven");
    } catch (e) {
        document.writeln(e.name + ': ' + e.message);
    }
}

try_it();
```

If an exception is thrown within a `try` block, control will go to its `catch` clause.

A `try` statement has a single `catch` block that will catch all exceptions. If your handling depends on the type of the exception, then the exception handler will have to inspect the `name` to determine the type of the exception.

# Augmenting Types

JavaScript allows the basic types of the language to be *augmented*. In Chapter 3, we saw that adding a method to `Object.prototype` makes that method available to all objects. This also works for functions, arrays, strings, numbers, regular expressions, and booleans.

For example, by augmenting `Function.prototype`, we can make a method available to all functions:

```
Function.prototype.method = function (name, func) {
    this.prototype[name] = func;
    return this;
};
```

By augmenting Function.prototype with a method method, we no longer have to type the name of the prototype property. That bit of ugliness can now be hidden.

JavaScript does not have a separate integer type, so it is sometimes necessary to extract just the integer part of a number. The method JavaScript provides to do that is ugly. We can fix it by adding an integer method to Number.prototype. It uses either Math.ceil or Math.floor, depending on the sign of the number:

```
Number.method('integer', function () {
    return Math[this < 0 ? 'ceil' : 'floor'](this);
});

document.writeln((-10 / 3).integer());  // -3
```

JavaScript lacks a method that removes spaces from the ends of a string. That is an easy oversight to fix:

```
String.method('trim', function () {
    return this.replace(/^\s+|\s+$/g, '');
});

document.writeln('"' + "   neat   ".trim() + '"');
```

Our trim method uses a regular expression. We will see much more about regular expressions in Chapter 7.

By augmenting the basic types, we can make significant improvements to the expressiveness of the language. Because of the dynamic nature of JavaScript's prototypal inheritance, all values are immediately endowed with the new methods, even values that were created before the methods were created.

The prototypes of the basic types are public structures, so care must be taken when mixing libraries. One defensive technique is to add a method only if the method is known to be missing:

```
// Add a method conditionally.

Function.prototype.method = function (name, func) {
    if (!this.prototype[name]) {
        this.prototype[name] = func;
        return this;
    }
};
```

Another concern is that the for in statement interacts badly with prototypes. We saw a couple of ways to mitigate that in Chapter 3: we can use the hasOwnProperty method to screen out inherited properties, and we can look for specific types.

# Recursion

A *recursive* function is a function that calls itself, either directly or indirectly. Recursion is a powerful programming technique in which a problem is divided into a set of similar subproblems, each solved with a trivial solution. Generally, a recursive function calls itself to solve its subproblems.

The Towers of Hanoi is a famous puzzle. The equipment includes three posts and a set of discs of various diameters with holes in their centers. The setup stacks all of the discs on the source post with smaller discs on top of larger discs. The goal is to move the stack to the destination post by moving one disc at a time to another post, never placing a larger disc on a smaller disc. This puzzle has a trivial recursive solution:

```
var hanoi = function hanoi(disc, src, aux, dst) {
    if (disc > 0) {
        hanoi(disc - 1, src, dst, aux);
        document.writeln('Move disc ' + disc +
                ' from ' + src + ' to ' + dst);
        hanoi(disc - 1, aux, src, dst);
    }
};

hanoi(3, 'Src', 'Aux', 'Dst');
```

It produces this solution for three discs:

```
Move disc 1 from Src to Dst
Move disc 2 from Src to Aux
Move disc 1 from Dst to Aux
Move disc 3 from Src to Dst
Move disc 1 from Aux to Src
Move disc 2 from Aux to Dst
Move disc 1 from Src to Dst
```

The hanoi function moves a stack of discs from one post to another, using the auxiliary post if necessary. It breaks the problem into three subproblems. First, it uncovers the bottom disc by moving the substack above it to the auxiliary post. It can then move the bottom disc to the destination post. Finally, it can move the substack from the auxiliary post to the destination post. The movement of the substack is handled by calling itself recursively to work out those subproblems.

The hanoi function is passed the number of the disc it is to move and the three posts it is to use. When it calls itself, it is to deal with the disc that is above the disc it is currently working on. Eventually, it will be called with a nonexistent disc number. In that case, it does nothing. That act of nothingness gives us confidence that the function does not recurse forever.

Recursive functions can be very effective in manipulating tree structures such as the browser's Document Object Model (DOM). Each recursive call is given a smaller piece of the tree to work on:

```
// Define a walk_the_DOM function that visits every
// node of the tree in HTML source order, starting
// from some given node. It invokes a function,
// passing it each node in turn. walk_the_DOM calls
// itself to process each of the child nodes.

var walk_the_DOM = function walk(node, func) {
    func(node);
    node = node.firstChild;
    while (node) {
        walk(node, func);
        node = node.nextSibling;
    }
};

// Define a getElementsByAttribute function. It
// takes an attribute name string and an optional
// matching value. It calls walk_the_DOM, passing it a
// function that looks for an attribute name in the
// node. The matching nodes are accumulated in a
// results array.

var getElementsByAttribute = function (att, value) {
    var results = [];

    walk_the_DOM(document.body, function (node) {
        var actual = node.nodeType === 1 && node.getAttribute(att);
        if (typeof actual === 'string' &&
                (actual === value || typeof value !== 'string')) {
            results.push(node);
        }
    });

    return results;
};
```

Some languages offer the *tail recursion optimization*. This means that if a function
returns the result of invoking itself recursively, then the invocation is replaced with a
loop, which can significantly speed things up. Unfortunately, JavaScript does not
currently provide tail recursion optimization. Functions that recurse very deeply can
fail by exhausting the return stack:

```
// Make a factorial function with tail
// recursion. It is tail recursive because
// it returns the result of calling itself.

// JavaScript does not currently optimize this form.

var factorial = function factorial(i, a) {
    a = a || 1;
    if (i < 2) {
        return a;
    }
    return factorial(i - 1, a * i);
```

```
    };

    document.writeln(factorial(4));      // 24
```

# Scope

*Scope* in a programming language controls the visibility and lifetimes of variables and parameters. This is an important service to the programmer because it reduces naming collisions and provides automatic memory management:

```
    var foo = function () {
        var a = 3, b = 5;

        var bar = function () {
            var b = 7, c = 11;

    // At this point, a is 3, b is 7, and c is 11

            a += b + c;

    // At this point, a is 21, b is 7, and c is 11

        };

    // At this point, a is 3, b is 5, and c is not defined

        bar();

    // At this point, a is 21, b is 5

    };
```

Most languages with C syntax have block scope. All variables defined in a block (a list of statements wrapped with curly braces) are not visible from outside of the block. The variables defined in a block can be released when execution of the block is finished. This is a good thing.

Unfortunately, JavaScript does not have block scope even though its block syntax suggests that it does. This confusion can be a source of errors.

JavaScript does have function scope. That means that the parameters and variables defined in a function are not visible outside of the function, and that a variable defined anywhere within a function is visible everywhere within the function.

In many modern languages, it is recommended that variables be declared as late as possible, at the first point of use. That turns out to be bad advice for JavaScript because it lacks block scope. So instead, it is best to declare all of the variables used in a function at the top of the function body.

# Closure

The good news about scope is that inner functions get access to the parameters and variables of the functions they are defined within (with the exception of this and arguments). This is a very good thing.

Our getElementsByAttribute function worked because it declared a results variable, and the inner function that it passed to walk_the_DOM also had access to the results variable.

A more interesting case is when the inner function has a longer lifetime than its outer function.

Earlier, we made a myObject that had a value and an increment method. Suppose we wanted to protect the value from unauthorized changes.

Instead of initializing myObject with an object literal, we will initialize myObject by calling a function that returns an object literal. That function defines a value variable. That variable is always available to the increment and getValue methods, but the function's scope keeps it hidden from the rest of the program:

```
var myObject = (function () {
    var value = 0;

    return {
        increment: function (inc) {
            value += typeof inc === 'number' ? inc : 1;
        },
        getValue: function () {
            return value;
        }
    };
}());
```

We are not assigning a function to myObject. We are assigning the result of invoking that function. Notice the ( ) on the last line. The function returns an object containing two methods, and those methods continue to enjoy the privilege of access to the value variable.

The Quo constructor from earlier in this chapter produced an object with a status property and a get_status method. But that doesn't seem very interesting. Why would you call a getter method on a property you could access directly? It would be more useful if the status property were private. So, let's define a different kind of quo function to do that:

```
// Create a maker function called quo. It makes an
// object with a get_status method and a private
// status property.
```

```
var quo = function (status) {
    return {
        get_status: function () {
            return status;
        }
    };
};

// Make an instance of quo.

var myQuo = quo("amazed");

document.writeln(myQuo.get_status());
```

This quo function is designed to be used without the new prefix, so the name is not capitalized. When we call quo, it returns a new object containing a get_status method. A reference to that object is stored in myQuo. The get_status method still has privileged access to quo's status property even though quo has already returned. get_status does not have access to a copy of the parameter; it has access to the parameter itself. This is possible because the function has access to the context in which it was created. This is called *closure*.

Let's look at a more useful example:

```
// Define a function that sets a DOM node's color
// to yellow and then fades it to white.

var fade = function (node) {
    var level = 1;
    var step = function () {
        var hex = level.toString(16);
        node.style.backgroundColor = '#FFFF' + hex + hex;
        if (level < 15) {
            level += 1;
            setTimeout(step, 100);
        }
    };
    setTimeout(step, 100);
};

fade(document.body);
```

We call fade, passing it document.body (the node created by the HTML <body> tag). fade sets level to 1. It defines a step function. It calls setTimeout, passing it the step function and a time (100 milliseconds). It then returns—fade has finished.

Suddenly, about a 10th of a second later, the step function gets invoked. It makes a base 16 character from fade's level. It then modifies the background color of fade's node. It then looks at fade's level. If it hasn't gotten to white yet, it then increments fade's level and uses setTimeout to schedule itself to run again.

Suddenly, the step function gets invoked again. But this time, fade's level is 2. fade returned a while ago, but its variables continue to live as long as they are needed by one or more of fade's inner functions.

It is important to understand that the inner function has access to the actual variables of the outer functions and not copies in order to avoid the following problem.

```
// BAD EXAMPLE

// Make a function that assigns event handler functions to an array of nodes the wrong way.
// When you click on a node, an alert box is supposed to display the ordinal of the node.
// But it always displays the number of nodes instead.

var add_the_handlers = function (nodes) {
    var i;
    for (i = 0; i < nodes.length; i += 1) {
        nodes[i].onclick = function (e) {
            alert(i);
        };
    }
};

// END BAD EXAMPLE
```

The add_the_handlers function was intended to give each handler a unique number i. It fails because the handler functions are bound to the variable i, not the value of the variable i at the time the function was made.

```
// BETTER EXAMPLE

// Make a function that assigns event handler functions to an array of nodes.
// When you click on a node, an alert box will display the ordinal of the node.

var add_the_handlers = function (nodes) {
    var helper = function (i) {
        return function (e) {
            alert(i);
        };
    };
    var i;
    for (i = 0; i < nodes.length; i += 1) {
        nodes[i].onclick = helper(i);
    }
};
```

Avoid creating functions within a loop. It can be wasteful computationally, and it can cause confusion, as we saw with the bad example. We avoid the confusion by creating a helper function outside of the loop that will deliver a function that binds to the current value of i.

# Callbacks

Functions can make it easier to deal with discontinuous events. For example, suppose there is a sequence that begins with a user interaction, making a request of the server, and finally displaying the server's response. The naïve way to write that would be:

```
request = prepare_the_request();
response = send_request_synchronously(request);
display(response);
```

The problem with this approach is that a synchronous request over the network will leave the client in a frozen state. If either the network or the server is slow, the degradation in responsiveness will be unacceptable.

A better approach is to make an asynchronous request, providing a callback function that will be invoked when the server's response is received. An asynchronous function returns immediately, so the client isn't blocked:

```
request = prepare_the_request();
send_request_asynchronously(request, function (response) {
    display(response);
});
```

We pass a function parameter to the send_request_asynchronously function that will be called when the response is available.

# Module

We can use functions and closure to make modules. A module is a function or object that presents an interface but that hides its state and implementation. By using functions to produce modules, we can almost completely eliminate our use of global variables, thereby mitigating one of JavaScript's worst features.

For example, suppose we want to augment String with a deentityify method. Its job is to look for HTML entities in a string and replace them with their equivalents. It makes sense to keep the names of the entities and their equivalents in an object. But where should we keep the object? We could put it in a global variable, but global variables are evil. We could define it in the function itself, but that has a runtime cost because the literal must be evaluated every time the function is invoked. The ideal approach is to put it in a closure, and perhaps provide an extra method that can add additional entities:

```
String.method('deentityify', function () {

// The entity table. It maps entity names to
// characters.

    var entity = {
        quot: '"',
```

```
            lt:    '<',
            gt:    '>'
        };

// Return the deentityify method.

        return function ( ) {

// This is the deentityify method. It calls the string
// replace method, looking for substrings that start
// with '&' and end with ';'. If the characters in
// between are in the entity table, then replace the
// entity with the character from the table. It uses
// a regular expression (Chapter 7).

            return this.replace(/&([^&;]+);/g,
                function (a, b) {
                    var r = entity[b];
                    return typeof r === 'string' ? r : a;
                }
            );
        };
    }());
```

Notice the last line. We immediately invoke the function we just made with the ( ) operator. That invocation creates and returns the function that becomes the deentityify method.

```
document.writeln(
    '&lt;&quot;&gt;'.deentityify( ));  // <">
```

The module pattern takes advantage of function scope and closure to create relationships that are binding and private. In this example, only the deentityify method has access to the entity data structure.

The general pattern of a module is a function that defines private variables and functions; creates privileged functions which, through closure, will have access to the private variables and functions; and that returns the privileged functions or stores them in an accessible place.

Use of the module pattern can eliminate the use of global variables. It promotes information hiding and other good design practices. It is very effective in encapsulating applications and other singletons.

It can also be used to produce objects that are secure. Let's suppose we want to make an object that produces a serial number:

```
var serial_maker = function ( ) {

// Produce an object that produces unique strings. A
// unique string is made up of two parts: a prefix
// and a sequence number. The object comes with
// methods for setting the prefix and sequence
```

```
// number, and a gensym method that produces unique
// strings.

    var prefix = '';
    var seq = 0;
    return {
        set_prefix: function (p) {
            prefix = String(p);
        },
        set_seq: function (s) {
            seq = s;
        },
        gensym: function () {
            var result = prefix + seq;
            seq += 1;
            return result;
        }
    };
};

var seqer = serial_maker();
seqer.set_prefix('Q');
seqer.set_seq(1000);
var unique = seqer.gensym();    // unique is "Q1000"
```

The methods do not make use of this or that. As a result, there is no way to compromise the seqer. It isn't possible to get or change the prefix or seq except as permitted by the methods. The seqer object is mutable, so the methods could be replaced, but that still does not give access to its secrets. seqer is simply a collection of functions, and those functions are capabilities that grant specific powers to use or modify the secret state.

If we passed seqer.gensym to a third party's function, that function would be able to generate unique strings, but would be unable to change the prefix or seq.

## Cascade

Some methods do not have a return value. For example, it is typical for methods that set or change the state of an object to return nothing. If we have those methods return this instead of undefined, we can enable *cascades*. In a cascade, we can call many methods on the same object in sequence in a single statement. An Ajax library that enables cascades would allow us to write in a style like this:

```
getElement('myBoxDiv')
    .move(350, 150)
    .width(100)
    .height(100)
    .color('red')
    .border('10px outset')
    .padding('4px')
    .appendText("Please stand by")
```

```
.on('mousedown', function (m) {
    this.startDrag(m, this.getNinth(m));
})
.on('mousemove', 'drag')
.on('mouseup', 'stopDrag')
.later(2000, function () {
    this
        .color('yellow')
        .setHTML("What hath God wraught?")
        .slide(400, 40, 200, 200);
})
tip('This box is resizeable');
```

In this example, the getElement function produces an object that gives functionality to the DOM element with id="myBoxDiv". The methods allow us to move the element, change its dimensions and styling, and add behavior. Each of those methods returns the object, so the result of the invocation can be used for the next invocation.

Cascading can produce interfaces that are very expressive. It can help control the tendency to make interfaces that try to do too much at once.

# Curry

Functions are values, and we can manipulate function values in interesting ways. *Currying* allows us to produce a new function by combining a function and an argument:

```
var add1 = add.curry(1);
document.writeln(add1(6));     // 7
```

add1 is a function that was created by passing 1 to add's curry method. The add1 function adds 1 to its argument. JavaScript does not have a curry method, but we can fix that by augmenting Function.prototype:

```
Function.method('curry', function () {
    var args = arguments, that = this;
    return function () {
        return that.apply(null, args.concat(arguments));
    };
});     // Something isn't right...
```

The curry method works by creating a closure that holds that original function and the arguments to curry. It returns a function that, when invoked, returns the result of calling that original function, passing it all of the arguments from the invocation of curry and the current invocation. It uses the Array concat method to concatenate the two arrays of arguments together.

Unfortunately, as we saw earlier, the arguments array is not an array, so it does not have the concat method. To work around that, we will apply the array slice method on both of the arguments arrays. This produces arrays that behave correctly with the concat method:

```
Function.method('curry', function () {
    var slice = Array.prototype.slice,
        args = slice.apply(arguments),
        that = this;
    return function () {
        return that.apply(null, args.concat(slice.apply(arguments)));
    };
});
```

# Memoization

Functions can use objects to remember the results of previous operations, making it possible to avoid unnecessary work. This optimization is called *memoization*. JavaScript's objects and arrays are very convenient for this.

Let's say we want a recursive function to compute Fibonacci numbers. A Fibonacci number is the sum of the two previous Fibonacci numbers. The first two are 0 and 1:

```
var fibonacci = function (n) {
    return n < 2 ? n : fibonacci(n - 1) + fibonacci(n - 2);
};

for (var i = 0; i <= 10; i += 1) {
    document.writeln('// ' + i + ': ' + fibonacci(i));
}

// 0: 0
// 1: 1
// 2: 1
// 3: 2
// 4: 3
// 5: 5
// 6: 8
// 7: 13
// 8: 21
// 9: 34
// 10: 55
```

This works, but it is doing a lot of unnecessary work. The `fibonacci` function is called 453 times. We call it 11 times, and it calls itself 442 times in computing values that were probably already recently computed. If we *memoize* the function, we can significantly reduce its workload.

We will keep our memoized results in a `memo` array that we can hide in a closure. When our function is called, it first looks to see if it already knows the result. If it does, it can immediately return it:

```
var fibonacci = (function () {
    var memo = [0, 1];
    var fib = function (n) {
        var result = memo[n];
        if (typeof result !== 'number') {
```

```
                result = fib(n - 1) + fib(n - 2);
                memo[n] = result;
            }
            return result;
        };
        return fib;
    }());
```

This function returns the same results, but it is called only 29 times. We called it 11 times. It called itself 18 times to obtain the previously memoized results.

We can generalize this by making a function that helps us make memoized functions. The memoizer function will take an initial memo array and the formula function. It returns a recur function that manages the memo store and that calls the formula function as needed. We pass the recur function and the function's parameters to the formula function:

```
var memoizer = function (memo, formula) {
    var recur = function (n) {
        var result = memo[n];
        if (typeof result !== 'number') {
            result = formula(recur, n);
            memo[n] = result;
        }
        return result;
    };
    return recur;
};
```

We can now define fibonacci with the memoizer, providing the initial memo array and formula function:

```
var fibonacci = memoizer([0, 1], function (recur, n) {
    return recur(n - 1) + recur(n - 2);
});
```

By devising functions that produce other functions, we can significantly reduce the amount of work we have to do. For example, to produce a memoizing factorial function, we only need to supply the basic factorial formula:

```
var factorial = memoizer([1, 1], function (recur, n) {
    return n * recur(n - 1);
});
```

# CHAPTER 5

# Inheritance

*Divides one thing entire to many objects;*
*Like perspectives, which rightly gazed upon*
*Show nothing but confusion...*
—William Shakespeare, *The Tragedy of King Richard the Second*

Inheritance is an important topic in most programming languages.

In the classical languages (such as Java), inheritance (or extends) provides two useful services. First, it is a form of code reuse. If a new class is mostly similar to an existing class, you only have to specify the differences. Patterns of code reuse are extremely important because they have the potential to significantly reduce the cost of software development. The other benefit of classical inheritance is that it includes the specification of a system of types. This mostly frees the programmer from having to write explicit casting operations, which is a very good thing because when casting, the safety benefits of a type system are lost.

JavaScript, being a loosely typed language, never casts. The lineage of an object is irrelevant. What matters about an object is what it can do, not what it is descended from.

JavaScript provides a much richer set of code reuse patterns. It can ape the classical pattern, but it also supports other patterns that are more expressive. The set of possible inheritance patterns in JavaScript is vast. In this chapter, we'll look at a few of the most straightforward patterns. Much more complicated constructions are possible, but it is usually best to keep it simple.

In classical languages, objects are instances of classes, and a class can inherit from another class. JavaScript is a prototypal language, which means that objects inherit directly from other objects.

# Pseudoclassical

JavaScript is conflicted about its prototypal nature. Its prototype mechanism is obscured by some complicated syntactic business that looks vaguely classical. Instead of having objects inherit directly from other objects, an unnecessary level of indirection is inserted such that objects are produced by constructor functions.

When a function object is created, the `Function` constructor that produces the function object runs some code like this:

```
this.prototype = {constructor: this};
```

The new function object is given a `prototype` property whose value is an object containing a `constructor` property whose value is the new function object. The `prototype` object is the place where inherited traits are to be deposited. Every function gets a `prototype` object because the language does not provide a way of determining which functions are intended to be used as constructors. The `constructor` property is not useful. It is the `prototype` object that is important.

When a function is invoked with the constructor invocation pattern using the `new` prefix, this modifies the way in which the function is executed. If the `new` operator were a method instead of an operator, it could have been implemented like this:

```
Function.method('new', function () {

// Create a new object that inherits from the
// constructor's prototype.

    var that = Object.create(this.prototype);

// Invoke the constructor, binding -this- to
// the new object.

    var other = this.apply(that, arguments);

// If its return value isn't an object,
// substitute the new object.

    return (typeof other === 'object' && other) || that;
});
```

We can define a constructor and augment its prototype:

```
var Mammal = function (name) {
    this.name = name;
};

Mammal.prototype.get_name = function () {
    return this.name;
};
```

```
Mammal.prototype.says = function ( ) {
    return this.saying || '';
};
```

Now, we can make an instance:

```
var myMammal = new Mammal('Herb the Mammal');
var name = myMammal.get_name( ); // 'Herb the Mammal'
```

We can make another pseudoclass that inherits from Mammal by defining its constructor function and replacing its prototype with an instance of Mammal:

```
var Cat = function (name) {
    this.name = name;
    this.saying = 'meow';
};

// Replace Cat.prototype with a new instance of Mammal

Cat.prototype = new Mammal( );

// Augment the new prototype with
// purr and get_name methods.

Cat.prototype.purr = function (n) {
    var i, s = '';
    for (i = 0; i < n; i += 1) {
        if (s) {
            s += '-';
        }
        s += 'r';
    }
    return s;
};
Cat.prototype.get_name = function ( ) {
    return this.says( ) + ' ' + this.name + ' ' + this.says( );
};

var myCat = new Cat('Henrietta');
var says = myCat.says( ); // 'meow'
var purr = myCat.purr(5); // 'r-r-r-r-r'
var name = myCat.get_name( );
//              'meow Henrietta meow'
```

The pseudoclassical pattern was intended to look sort of object-oriented, but it is looking quite alien. We can hide some of the ugliness by using the method method and defining an inherits method:

```
Function.method('inherits', function (Parent) {
    this.prototype = new Parent( );
    return this;
});
```

Our inherits and method methods return this, allowing us to program in a cascade style. We can now make our Cat with one statement.

```
var Cat = function (name) {
    this.name = name;
    this.saying = 'meow';
}.
    inherits(Mammal).
    method('purr', function (n) {
        var i, s = '';
        for (i = 0; i < n; i += 1) {
            if (s) {
                s += '-';
            }
            s += 'r';
        }
        return s;
    }).
    method('get_name', function () {
        return this.says() + ' ' + this.name + ' ' + this.says();
    });
```

By hiding the prototype jazz, it now looks a bit less alien. But have we really improved anything? We now have constructor functions that act like classes, but at the edges, there may be surprising behavior. There is no privacy; all properties are public. There is no access to super methods.

Even worse, there is a serious hazard with the use of constructor functions. If you forget to include the new prefix when calling a constructor function, then this will not be bound to a new object. Sadly, this will be bound to the global object, so instead of augmenting your new object, you will be clobbering global variables. That is really bad. There is no compile warning, and there is no runtime warning.

This is a serious design error in the language. To mitigate this problem, there is a convention that all constructor functions are named with an initial capital, and that nothing else is spelled with an initial capital. This gives us a prayer that visual inspection can find a missing new. A much better alternative is to not use new at all.

The pseudoclassical form can provide comfort to programmers who are unfamiliar with JavaScript, but it also hides the true nature of the language. The classically inspired notation can induce programmers to compose hierarchies that are unnecessarily deep and complicated. Much of the complexity of class hierarchies is motivated by the constraints of static type checking. JavaScript is completely free of those constraints. In classical languages, class inheritance is the only form of code reuse. JavaScript has more and better options.

# Object Specifiers

It sometimes happens that a constructor is given a very large number of parameters. This can be troublesome because it can be very difficult to remember the order of the arguments. In such cases, it can be much friendlier if we write the constructor to accept a single object specifier instead. That object contains the specification of the object to be constructed. So, instead of:

```
var myObject = maker(f, l, m, c, s);
```

we can write:

```
var myObject = maker({
    first: f,
    last: l,
    middle: m,
    state: s,
    city: c
});
```

The arguments can now be listed in any order, arguments can be left out if the constructor is smart about defaults, and the code is much easier to read.

This can have a secondary benefit when working with JSON (see Appendix E). JSON text can only describe data, but sometimes the data represents an object, and it would be useful to associate the data with its methods. This can be done trivially if the constructor takes an object specifier because we can simply pass the JSON object to the constructor and it will return a fully constituted object.

# Prototypal

In a purely prototypal pattern, we dispense with classes. We focus instead on the objects. Prototypal inheritance is conceptually simpler than classical inheritance: a new object can inherit the properties of an old object. This is perhaps unfamiliar, but it is really easy to understand. You start by making a useful object. You can then make many more objects that are like that one. The classification process of breaking an application down into a set of nested abstract classes can be completely avoided.

Let's start by using an object literal to make a useful object:

```
var myMammal = {
    name : 'Herb the Mammal',
    get_name : function () {
        return this.name;
    },
    says : function () {
        return this.saying || '';
    }
};
```

Once we have an object that we like, we can make more instances with the `Object.create` method from Chapter 3. We can then customize the new instances:

```javascript
var myCat = Object.create(myMammal);
myCat.name = 'Henrietta';
myCat.saying = 'meow';
myCat.purr = function (n) {
    var i, s = '';
    for (i = 0; i < n; i += 1) {
        if (s) {
            s += '-';
        }
        s += 'r';
    }
    return s;
};
myCat.get_name = function () {
    return this.says() + ' ' + this.name + ' ' + this.says();
};
```

This is *differential inheritance*. By customizing a new object, we specify the differences from the object on which it is based.

Sometimes is it useful for data structures to inherit from other data structures. Here is an example: Suppose we are parsing a language such as JavaScript or T$_E$X in which a pair of curly braces indicates a scope. Items defined in a scope are not visible outside of the scope. In a sense, an inner scope inherits from its outer scope. JavaScript objects are very good at representing this relationship. The `block` function is called when a left curly brace is encountered. The `parse` function will look up symbols from scope, and augment scope when it defines new symbols:

```javascript
var block = function () {

// Remember the current scope. Make a new scope that
// includes everything from the current one.

    var oldScope = scope;
    scope = Object.create(scope);

// Advance past the left curly brace.

    advance('{');

// Parse using the new scope.

    parse(scope);

// Advance past the right curly brace and discard the
// new scope, restoring the old one.

    advance('}');
    scope = oldScope;
};
```

# Functional

One weakness of the inheritance patterns we have seen so far is that we get no privacy. All properties of an object are visible. We get no private variables and no private methods. Sometimes that doesn't matter, but sometimes it matters a lot. In frustration, some uninformed programmers have adopted a pattern of *pretend privacy*. If they have a property that they wish to make private, they give it an odd-looking name, with the hope that other users of the code will pretend that they cannot see the odd looking members. Fortunately, we have a much better alternative in an application of the module pattern.

We start by making a function that will produce objects. We will give it a name that starts with a lowercase letter because it will not require the use of the new prefix. The function contains four steps:

1. It creates a new object. There are lots of ways to make an object. It can make an object literal, or it can call a constructor function with the new prefix, or it can use the Object.create method to make a new instance from an existing object, or it can call any function that returns an object.

2. It optionally defines private instance variables and methods. These are just ordinary vars of the function.

3. It augments that new object with methods. Those methods will have privileged access to the parameters and the vars defined in the second step.

4. It returns that new object.

Here is a pseudocode template for a functional constructor (boldface text added for emphasis):

```
var constructor = function (spec, my) {
    var that, other private instance variables;
    my = my || {};

    Add shared variables and functions to my

    that = a new object;

    Add privileged methods to that

    return that;
};
```

The spec object contains all of the information that the constructor needs to make an instance. The contents of the spec could be copied into private variables or transformed by other functions. Or the methods can access information from spec as they need it. (A simplification is to replace spec with a single value. This is useful when the object being constructed does not need a whole spec object.)

The my object is a container of secrets that are shared by the constructors in the inheritance chain. The use of the my object is optional. If a my object is not passed in, then a my object is made.

Next, declare the private instance variables and private methods for the object. This is done by simply declaring variables. The variables and inner functions of the constructor become the private members of the instance. The inner functions have access to spec and my and that and the private variables.

Next, add the shared secrets to the my object. This is done by assignment:

```
my.member = value;
```

Now, we make a new object and assign it to that. There are lots of ways to make a new object. We can use an object literal. We can call a pseudoclassical constructor with the new operator. We can use the Object.create method on a prototype object. Or, we can call another functional constructor, passing it a spec object (possibly the same spec object that was passed to this constructor) and the my object. The my object allows the other constructor to share the material that we put into my. The other constructor may also put its own shared secrets into my so that our constructor can take advantage of it.

Next, we augment that, adding the privileged methods that make up the object's interface. We can assign new functions to members of that. Or, more securely, we can define the functions first as private methods, and then assign them to that:

```
var methodical = function ( ) {
    ...
};
that.methodical = methodical;
```

The advantage to defining methodical in two steps is that if other methods want to call methodical, they can call methodical() instead of that.methodical(). If the instance is damaged or tampered with so that that.methodical is replaced, the methods that call methodical will continue to work the same because their private methodical is not affected by modification of the instance.

Finally, we return that.

Let's apply this pattern to our mammal example. We don't need my here, so we'll just leave it out, but we will use a spec object.

The name and saying properties are now completely private. They are accessible only via the privileged get_name and says methods:

```
var mammal = function (spec) {
    var that = {};

    that.get_name = function ( ) {
        return spec.name;
    };
```

```
    that.says = function () {
        return spec.saying || '';
    };

    return that;
};

var myMammal = mammal({name: 'Herb'});
```

In the pseudoclassical pattern, the Cat constructor function had to duplicate work that was done by the Mammal constructor. That isn't necessary in the functional pattern because the Cat constructor will call the Mammal constructor, letting Mammal do most of the work of object creation, so Cat only has to concern itself with the differences:

```
var cat = function (spec) {
    spec.saying = spec.saying || 'meow';
    var that = mammal(spec);
    that.purr = function (n) {
        var i, s = '';
        for (i = 0; i < n; i += 1) {
            if (s) {
                s += '-';
            }
            s += 'r';
        }
        return s;
    };
    that.get_name = function () {
        return that.says() + ' ' + spec.name + ' ' + that.says();
    };
    return that;
};

var myCat = cat({name: 'Henrietta'});
```

The functional pattern also gives us a way to deal with super methods. We will make a superior method that takes a method name and returns a function that invokes that method. The function will invoke the original method even if the property is changed:

```
Object.method('superior', function (name) {
    var that = this,
        method = that[name];
    return function () {
        return method.apply(that, arguments);
    };
});
```

Let's try it out on a coolcat that is just like cat except it has a cooler get_name method that calls the super method. It requires just a little bit of preparation. We will declare a super_get_name variable and assign it the result of invoking the superior method:

```
var coolcat = function (spec) {
    var that = cat(spec),
        super_get_name = that.superior('get_name');
    that.get_name = function (n) {
        return 'like ' + super_get_name() + ' baby';
    };
    return that;
};

var myCoolCat = coolcat({name: 'Bix'});
var name = myCoolCat.get_name( );
//          'like meow Bix meow baby'
```

The functional pattern has a great deal of flexibility. It requires less effort than the pseudoclassical pattern, and gives us better encapsulation and information hiding and access to super methods.

If all of the state of an object is private, then the object is tamper-proof. Properties of the object can be replaced or deleted, but the integrity of the object is not compromised. If we create an object in the functional style, and if all of the methods of the object make no use of this or that, then the object is *durable*. A durable object is simply a collection of functions that act as *capabilities*.

A durable object cannot be compromised. Access to a durable object does not give an attacker the ability to access the internal state of the object except as permitted by the methods.

# Parts

We can compose objects out of sets of parts. For example, we can make a function that can add simple event processing features to any object. It adds an on method, a fire method, and a private event registry:

```
var eventuality = function (that) {
    var registry = {};

    that.fire = function (event) {

// Fire an event on an object. The event can be either
// a string containing the name of the event or an
// object containing a type property containing the
// name of the event. Handlers registered by the 'on'
// method that match the event name will be invoked.

        var array,
            func,
            handler,
            i,
            type = typeof event === 'string' ? event : event.type;
```

```
// If an array of handlers exist for this event, then
// loop through it and execute the handlers in order.

        if (registry.hasOwnProperty(type)) {
            array = registry[type];
            for (i = 0; i < array.length; i += 1) {
                handler = array[i];

// A handler record contains a method and an optional
// array of parameters. If the method is a name, look
// up the function.

                func = handler.method;
                if (typeof func === 'string') {
                    func = this[func];
                }

// Invoke a handler. If the record contained
// parameters, then pass them. Otherwise, pass the
// event object.

                func.apply(this,
                    handler.parameters || [event]);
            }
        }
        return this;
    };

    that.on = function (type, method, parameters) {

// Register an event. Make a handler record. Put it
// in a handler array, making one if it doesn't yet
// exist for this type.

        var handler = {
            method: method,
            parameters: parameters
        };
        if (registry.hasOwnProperty(type)) {
            registry[type].push(handler);
        } else {
            registry[type] = [handler];
        }
        return this;
    };
    return that;
};
```

We could call eventuality on any individual object, bestowing it with event handling methods. We could also call it in a constructor function before that is returned:

```
eventuality(that);
```

In this way, a constructor could assemble objects from a set of parts. JavaScript's loose typing is a big benefit here because we are not burdened with a type system that is concerned about the lineage of classes. Instead, we can focus on the character of their contents.

If we wanted eventuality to have access to the object's private state, we could pass it the my bundle.

# CHAPTER 6

# Arrays

*Thee I'll chase hence, thou wolf in sheep's array.*
—William Shakespeare, *The First Part of Henry the Sixth*

An *array* is a linear allocation of memory in which elements are accessed by integers that are used to compute offsets. Arrays can be very fast data structures. Unfortunately, JavaScript does not have anything like this kind of array.

Instead, JavaScript provides an object that has some array-like characteristics. It converts array subscripts into strings that are used to make properties. It is significantly slower than a real array, but it can be more convenient to use. Retrieval and updating of properties work the same as with objects, except that there is a special trick with integer property names. Arrays have their own literal format. Arrays also have a much more useful set of built-in methods, described in Chapter 8.

## Array Literals

Array literals provide a very convenient notation for creating new array values. An array literal is a pair of square brackets surrounding zero or more values separated by commas. An array literal can appear anywhere an expression can appear. The first value will get the property name '0', the second value will get the property name '1', and so on:

```
var empty = [];
var numbers = [
    'zero', 'one', 'two', 'three', 'four',
    'five', 'six', 'seven', 'eight', 'nine'
];

empty[1]          // undefined
numbers[1]        // 'one'

empty.length      // 0
numbers.length    // 10
```

The object literal:

```
var numbers_object = {
    '0': 'zero',  '1': 'one',   '2': 'two',
    '3': 'three', '4': 'four',  '5': 'five',
    '6': 'six',   '7': 'seven', '8': 'eight',
    '9': 'nine'
};
```

produces a similar result. Both numbers and numbers_object are objects containing 10 properties, and those properties have exactly the same names and values. But there are also significant differences. numbers inherits from Array.prototype, whereas numbers_object inherits from Object.prototype, so numbers inherits a larger set of useful methods. Also, numbers gets the mysterious length property, while numbers_object does not.

In most languages, the elements of an array are all required to be of the same type. JavaScript allows an array to contain any mixture of values:

```
var misc = [
    'string', 98.6, true, false, null, undefined,
    ['nested', 'array'], {object: true}, NaN,
    Infinity
];
misc.length    // 10
```

# Length

Every array has a length property. Unlike most other languages, JavaScript's array length is not an upper bound. If you store an element with a subscript that is greater than or equal to the current length, the length will increase to contain the new element. There is no array bounds error.

The length property is the largest integer property name in the array plus one. This is not necessarily the number of properties in the array:

```
var myArray = [];
myArray.length              // 0

myArray[1000000] = true;
myArray.length              // 1000001
// myArray contains one property.
```

The [] postfix subscript operator converts its expression to a string using the expression's toString method if it has one. That string will be used as the property name. If the string looks like a positive integer that is greater than or equal to the array's current length and is less than 4,294,967,295, then the length of the array is set to the new subscript plus one.

The length can be set explicitly. Making the length larger does not allocate more space for the array. Making the length smaller will cause all properties with a subscript that is greater than or equal to the new length to be deleted:

```
numbers.length = 3;
// numbers is ['zero', 'one', 'two']
```

A new element can be appended to the end of an array by assigning to the array's current length:

```
numbers[numbers.length] = 'shi';
// numbers is ['zero', 'one', 'two', 'shi']
```

It is sometimes more convenient to use the push method to accomplish the same thing:

```
numbers.push('go');
// numbers is ['zero', 'one', 'two', 'shi', 'go']
```

## Delete

Since JavaScript's arrays are really objects, the delete operator can be used to remove elements from an array:

```
delete numbers[2];
// numbers is ['zero', 'one', undefined, 'shi', 'go']
```

Unfortunately, that leaves a hole in the array. This is because the elements to the right of the deleted element retain their original names. What you usually want is to decrement the names of each of the elements to the right.

Fortunately, JavaScript arrays have a splice method. It can do surgery on an array, deleting some number of elements and replacing them with other elements. The first argument is an ordinal in the array. The second argument is the number of elements to delete. Any additional arguments get inserted into the array at that point:

```
numbers.splice(2, 1);
// numbers is ['zero', 'one', 'shi', 'go']
```

The property whose value is 'shi' has its key changed from '3' to '2'. Because every property after the deleted property must be removed and reinserted with a new key, this might not go quickly for large arrays.

## Enumeration

Since JavaScript's arrays are really objects, the for in statement can be used to iterate over all of the properties of an array. Unfortunately, for in makes no guarantee about the order of the properties, and most array applications expect the elements to be produced in numerical order. Also, there is still the problem with unexpected properties being dredged up from the prototype chain.

Fortunately, the conventional for statement avoids these problems. JavaScript's for statement is similar to that in most C-like languages. It is controlled by three clauses—the first initializes the loop, the second is the while condition, and the third does the increment:

```
var i;
for (i = 0; i < myArray.length; i += 1) {
    document.writeln(myArray[i]);
}
```

## Confusion

A common error in JavaScript programs is to use an object when an array is required or an array when an object is required. The rule is simple: when the property names are small sequential integers, you should use an array. Otherwise, use an object.

JavaScript itself is confused about the difference between arrays and objects. The typeof operator reports that the type of an array is 'object', which isn't very helpful.

JavaScript does not have a good mechanism for distinguishing between arrays and objects. We can work around that deficiency by defining our own is_array function:

```
var is_array = function (value) {
    return value && typeof value === 'object' && value.constructor === Array;
};
```

Unfortunately, it fails to identify arrays that were constructed in a different window or frame. If we want to accurately detect those foreign arrays, we have to work a little harder:

```
var is_array = function (value) {
    return Object.prototype.toString.apply(value) === '[object Array]';
};
```

## Methods

JavaScript provides a set of methods for acting on arrays. The methods are functions stored in Array.prototype. In Chapter 3, we saw that Object.prototype can be augmented. Array.prototype can be augmented as well.

For example, suppose we want to add an array method that will allow us to do computation on an array:

```
Array.method('reduce', function (f, value) {
    var i;
    for (i = 0; i < this.length; i += 1) {
        value = f(this[i], value);
    }
    return value;
});
```

By adding a function to `Array.prototype`, every array inherits the method. In this case, we defined a reduce method that takes a function and a starting value. For each element of the array, it calls the function with an element and the value, and computes a new value. When it is finished, it returns the value. If we pass in a function that adds two numbers, it computes the sum. If we pass in a function that multiplies two numbers, it computes the product:

```
// Create an array of numbers.

var data = [4, 8, 15, 16, 23, 42];

// Define two simple functions. One will add two
// numbers. The other will multiply two numbers.

var add = function (a, b) {
    return a + b;
};

var mult = function (a, b) {
    return a * b;
};

// Invoke the data's reduce method, passing in the
// add function.

var sum = data.reduce(add, 0);     // sum is 108

// Invoke the reduce method again, this time passing
// in the multiply function.

var product = data.reduce(mult, 1);
    // product is 7418880
```

Because an array is really an object, we can add methods directly to an individual array:

```
// Give the data array a total function.

data.total = function () {
    return this.reduce(add, 0);
};

total = data.total();     // total is 108
```

Since the string `'total'` is not an integer, adding a total property to an array does not change its length. Arrays are most useful when the property names are integers, but they are still objects, and objects can accept any string as a property name.

It is not useful to use the `Object.create` method from Chapter 3 on arrays because it produces an object, not an array. The object produced will inherit the array's values and methods, but it will not have the special length property.

# Dimensions

JavaScript arrays usually are not initialized. If you ask for a new array with [ ], it will be empty. If you access a missing element, you will get the undefined value. If you are aware of that, or if you will naturally set every element before you attempt to retrieve it, then all is well. But if you are implementing algorithms that assume that every element starts with a known value (such as 0), then you must prep the array yourself. JavaScript should have provided some form of an `Array.dim` method to do this, but we can easily correct this oversight:

```
Array.dim = function (dimension, initial) {
    var a = [], i;
    for (i = 0; i < dimension; i += 1) {
        a[i] = initial;
    }
    return a;
};

// Make an array containing 10 zeros.

var myArray = Array.dim(10, 0);
```

JavaScript does not have arrays of more than one dimension, but like most C languages, it can have arrays of arrays:

```
var matrix = [
    [0, 1, 2],
    [3, 4, 5],
    [6, 7, 8]
];
matrix[2][1]    // 7
```

To make a two-dimensional array or an array of arrays, you must build the arrays yourself:

```
for (i = 0; i < n; i += 1) {
    my_array[i] = [];
}

// Note: Array.dim(n, []) will not work here.
// Each element would get a reference to the same
// array, which would be very bad.
```

The cells of an empty matrix will initially have the value undefined. If you want them to have a different initial value, you must explicitly set them. Again, JavaScript should have provided better support for matrixes. We can correct that, too:

```
Array.matrix = function (m, n, initial) {
    var a, i, j, mat = [];
    for (i = 0; i < m; i += 1) {
        a = [];
        for (j = 0; j < n; j += 1) {
            a[j] = initial;
        }
        mat[i] = a;
```

```
    }
    return mat;
};

// Make a 4 * 4 matrix filled with zeros.

var myMatrix = Array.matrix(4, 4, 0);

document.writeln(myMatrix[3][3]);    // 0

// Method to make an identity matrix.

Array.identity = function (n) {
    var i, mat = Array.matrix(n, n, 0);
    for (i = 0; i < n; i += 1) {
        mat[i][i] = 1;
    }
    return mat;
};

myMatrix = Array.identity(4);

document.writeln(myMatrix[3][3]);    // 1
```

# CHAPTER 7

# Regular Expressions

*Whereas the contrary bringeth bliss,*
*And is a pattern of celestial peace.*
*Whom should we match with Henry, being a king...*
—William Shakespeare, *The First Part of Henry the Sixth*

Many of JavaScript's features were borrowed from other languages. The syntax came from Java, functions came from Scheme, and prototypal inheritance came from Self. JavaScript's Regular Expression feature was borrowed from Perl.

A *regular expression* is the specification of the syntax of a simple language. Regular expressions are used with methods to search, replace, and extract information from strings. The methods that work with regular expressions are regexp.exec, regexp.test, string.match, string.replace, string.search, and string.split. These will all be described in Chapter 8. Regular expressions usually have a significant performance advantage over equivalent string operations in JavaScript.

Regular expressions came from the mathematical study of formal languages. Ken Thompson adapted Stephen Kleene's theoretical work on type-3 languages into a practical pattern matcher that could be embedded in tools such as text editors and programming languages.

The syntax of regular expressions in JavaScript conforms closely to the original formulations from Bell Labs, with some reinterpretation and extension adopted from Perl. The rules for writing regular expressions can be surprisingly complex because they interpret characters in some positions as operators, and in slightly different positions as literals. Worse than being hard to write, this makes regular expressions hard to read and dangerous to modify. It is necessary to have a fairly complete understanding of the full complexity of regular expressions to correctly read them. To mitigate this, I have simplified the rules a little. As presented here, regular expressions will be slightly less terse, but they will also be slightly easier to use correctly. And that is a good thing because regular expressions can be very difficult to maintain and debug.

Today's regular expressions are not strictly regular, but they can be very useful. Regular expressions tend to be extremely terse, even cryptic. They are easy to use in their simplest form, but they can quickly become bewildering. JavaScript's regular expressions are difficult to read in part because they do not allow comments or whitespace. All of the parts of a regular expression are pushed tightly together, making them almost indecipherable. This is a particular concern when they are used in security applications for scanning and validation. If you cannot read and understand a regular expression, how can you have confidence that it will work correctly for all inputs? Yet, despite their obvious drawbacks, regular expressions are widely used.

## An Example

Here is an example. It is a regular expression that matches URLs. The pages of this book are not infinitely wide, so I broke it into two lines. In a JavaScript program, the regular expression must be on a single line. Whitespace is significant:

```
var parse_url = /^(?:([A-Za-z]+):)?(\/\/{0,3})([0-9.\-A-Za-z]+)
(?::(\d+))?(?:\/([^?#]*))?(?:\?([^#]*))?(?:#(.*))?$/;

var url = "http://www.ora.com:80/goodparts?q#fragment";
```

Let's call parse_url's exec method. If it successfully matches the string that we pass it, it will return an array containing pieces extracted from the url:

```
var url = "http://www.ora.com:80/goodparts?q#fragment";

var result = parse_url.exec(url);

var names = ['url', 'scheme', 'slash', 'host', 'port',
    'path', 'query', 'hash'];

var blanks = '         ';
var i;

for (i = 0; i < names.length; i += 1) {
    document.writeln(names[i] + ':' +
        blanks.substring(names[i].length), result[i]);
}
```

This produces:

```
url:     http://www.ora.com:80/goodparts?q#fragment
scheme: http
slash:  //
host:   www.ora.com
port:   80
path:   goodparts
query:  q
hash:   fragment
```

In Chapter 2, we used railroad diagrams to describe the JavaScript language. We can also use them to describe the languages defined by regular expressions. That may make it easier to see what a regular expression does. This is a railroad diagram for parse_url.

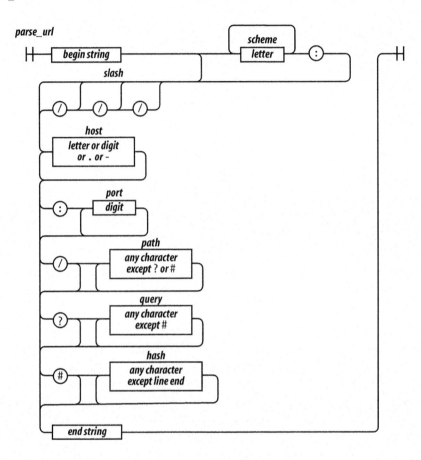

Regular expressions cannot be broken into smaller pieces the way that functions can, so the track representing parse_url is a long one.

Let's factor parse_url into its parts to see how it works.

```
^
```

The ^ character indicates the beginning of the string. It is an anchor that prevents exec from skipping over a non-URL-like prefix.

```
(?:([A-Za-z]+):)?
```

This factor matches a scheme name, but only if it is followed by a : (colon). The (?: ...) indicates a noncapturing group. The suffix ? indicates that the group is optional.

It means *repeat zero or one time*. The (…) indicates a capturing group. A capturing group copies the text it matches and places it in the result array. Each capturing group is given a number. This first capturing group is 1, so a copy of the text matched by this capturing group will appear in result[1]. The […] indicates a character class. This character class, A-Za-z, contains 26 uppercase letters and 26 lowercase letters. The hyphens indicate ranges, from A to Z. The suffix + indicates that the character class will be matched one or more times. The group is followed by the : character, which will be matched literally.

    (\/{0,3})

The next factor is capturing group 2. \/ indicates that a / (slash) character should be matched. It is escaped with \ (backslash) so that it is not misinterpreted as the end of the regular expression literal. The suffix {0,3} indicates that the / will be matched 0 or 1 or 2 or 3 times.

    ([0-9.\-A-Za-z]+)

The next factor is capturing group 3. It will match a host name, which is made up of one or more digits, letters, or . or -. The - was escaped as \- to prevent it from being confused with a range hyphen.

    (?::(\d+))?

The next factor optionally matches a port number, which is a sequence of one or more digits preceded by a :. \d represents a digit character. The series of one or more digits will be capturing group 4.

    (?:\/([^?#]*))?

We have another optional group. This one begins with a /. The character class [^?#] begins with a ^, which indicates that the class includes all characters *except ? and #*. The * indicates that the character class is matched zero or more times.

Note that I am being sloppy here. The class of all characters *except ? and #* includes line-ending characters, control characters, and lots of other characters that really shouldn't be matched here. Most of the time this will do what we want, but there is a risk that some bad text could slip through. Sloppy regular expressions are a popular source of security exploits. It is a lot easier to write sloppy regular expressions than rigorous regular expressions.

    (?:\?([^#]*))?

Next, we have an optional group that begins with a ?. It contains capturing group 6, which contains zero or more characters that are not #.

    (?:#(.*))?

We have a final optional group that begins with #. The . will match any character except a line-ending character.

    $

The $ represents the end of the string. It assures us that there was no extra material after the end of the URL.

Those are the factors of the regular expression parse_url.[*]

It is possible to make regular expressions that are more complex than parse_url, but I wouldn't recommend it. Regular expressions are best when they are short and simple. Only then can we have confidence that they are working correctly and that they could be successfully modified if necessary.

There is a very high degree of compatibility between JavaScript language processors. The part of the language that is *least* portable is the implementation of regular expressions. Regular expressions that are very complicated or convoluted are more likely to have portability problems. Nested regular expressions can also suffer horrible performance problems in some implementations. Simplicity is the best strategy.

Let's look at another example: a regular expression that matches numbers. Numbers can have an integer part with an optional minus sign, an optional fractional part, and an optional exponent part.

```
var parse_number = /^-?\d+(?:\.\d*)?(?:e[+\-]?\d+)?$/i;

var test = function (num) {
    document.writeln(parse_number.test(num));
};

test('1');                  // true
test('number');             // false
test('98.6');               // true
test('132.21.86.100');      // false
test('123.45E-67');         // true
test('123.45D-67');         // false
```

parse_number successfully identified the strings that conformed to our specification and those that did not, but for those that did not, it gives us no information on why or where they failed the number test.

Let's break down parse_number.

```
/^    $/i
```

We again use ^ and $ to anchor the regular expression. This causes all of the characters in the text to be matched against the regular expression. If we had omitted the anchors, the regular expression would tell us if a string contains a number. With the anchors, it tells us if the string contains only a number. If we included just the ^, it would match strings starting with a number. If we included just the $, it would match strings ending with a number.

---

[*] When you press them all together again, it is visually quite confusing:
```
/^(?:([A-Za-z]+):)?(\/{0,3})([0-9.\-A-Za-z]+)(?::(\d+))?(?:\/([^?#]*))?(?:\?([^#]*))?(?:#(.*))?$/
```

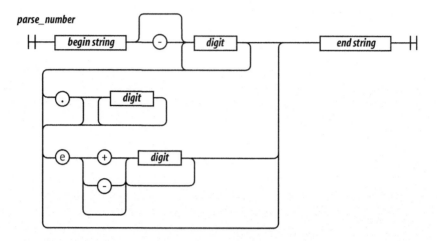

parse_number

The i flag causes case to be ignored when matching letters. The only letter in our pattern is e. We want that e to also match E. We could have written the e factor as [Ee] or (?:E|e), but we didn't have to because we used the i flag.

```
-?
```

The ? suffix on the minus sign indicates that the minus sign is optional.

```
\d+
```

\d means the same as [0-9]. It matches a digit. The + suffix causes it to match one or more digits.

```
(?:\.\d*)?
```

The (?:...)? indicates an optional noncapturing group. It is usually better to use noncapturing groups instead of the less ugly capturing groups because capturing has a performance penalty. The group will match a decimal point followed by zero or more digits.

```
(?:e[+\-]?\d+)?
```

This is another optional noncapturing group. It matches e (or E), an optional sign, and one or more digits.

# Construction

There are two ways to make a RegExp object. The preferred way, as we saw in the examples, is to use a regular expression literal.

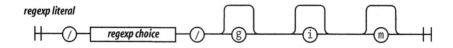

regexp literal

Regular expression literals are enclosed in slashes. This can be a little tricky because slash is also used as the division operator and in comments.

There are three flags that can be set on a RegExp. They are indicated by the letters g, i, and m, as listed in Table 7-1. The flags are appended directly to the end of the RegExp literal:

```
// Make a regular expression object that matches
// a JavaScript string.

var my_regexp = /"(?:\\.|[^\\\"])*"/g;
```

Table 7-1. Flags for regular expressions

| Flag | Meaning |
| --- | --- |
| g | Global (match multiple times; the precise meaning of this varies with the method) |
| i | Insensitive (ignore character case) |
| m | Multiline (^ and $ can match line-ending characters) |

The other way to make a regular expression is to use the RegExp constructor. The constructor takes a string and compiles it into a RegExp object. Some care must be taken in building the string because backslashes have a somewhat different meaning in regular expressions than in string literals. It is usually necessary to double the backslashes and escape the quotes:

```
// Make a regular expression object that matches
// a JavaScript string.

var my_regexp = new RegExp("'(?:\\\\.|[^\\\\\\'])*'", 'g'));
```

The second parameter is a string specifying the flags. The RegExp constructor is useful when a regular expression must be generated at runtime using material that is not available to the programmer.

RegExp objects contain the properties listed in Table 7-2.

Table 7-2. Properties of RegExp objects

| Property | Use |
| --- | --- |
| global | true if the g flag was used. |
| ignoreCase | true if the i flag was used. |
| lastIndex | The index at which to start the next exec match. Initially it is zero. |
| multiline | true if the m flag was used. |
| source | The source text of the regular expression. |

RegExp objects made by regular expression literals share a single instance:

```
function make_a_matcher( ) {
    return /a/gi;
}

var x = make_a_matcher( );
var y = make_a_matcher( );

// Beware: x and y are the same object!

x.lastIndex = 10;

document.writeln(y.lastIndex);    // 10
```

# Elements

Let's look more closely at the elements that make up regular expressions.

## Regexp Choice

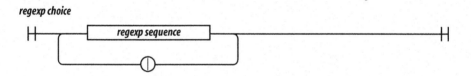

A *regexp choice* contains one or more *regexp sequences*. The sequences are separated by the | (vertical bar) character. The choice matches if any of the sequences match. It attempts to match each of the sequences in order. So:

```
"into".match(/in|int/)
```

matches the in in into. It wouldn't match int because the match of in was successful.

## Regexp Sequence

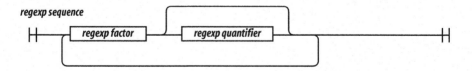

A *regexp sequence* contains one or more *regexp factors*. Each factor can optionally be followed by a quantifier that determines how many times the factor is allowed to appear. If there is no quantifier, then the factor will be matched one time.

# Regexp Factor

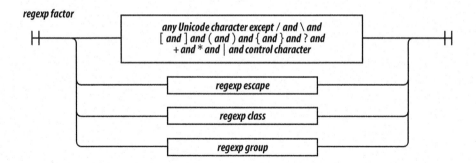

A *regexp factor* can be a character, a parenthesized group, a character class, or an escape sequence. All characters are treated literally except for the control characters and the special characters:

    \ / [ ] ( ) { } ? + * | . ^ $

which must be escaped with a \ prefix if they are to be matched literally. When in doubt, any special character can be given a \ prefix to make it literal. The \ prefix *does not* make letters or digits literal.

An unescaped . matches any character except a line-ending character.

An unescaped ^ matches the beginning of the text when the lastIndex property is zero. It can also match line-ending characters when the m flag is specified.

An unescaped $ matches the end of the text. It can also match line-ending characters when the m flag is specified.

# Regexp Escape

The backslash character indicates escapement in regexp factors as well as in strings, but in regexp factors, it works a little differently.

As in strings, \f is the formfeed character, \n is the newline character, \r is the carriage return character, \t is the tab character, and \u allows for specifying a Unicode character as a 16-bit hex constant. In regexp factors, \b *is not* the backspace character.

\d is the same as [0-9]. It matches a digit. \D is the opposite: [^0-9].

\s is the same as [\f\n\r\t\u000B\u0020\u00A0\u2028\u2029]. This is a partial set of Unicode whitespace characters. \S is the opposite: [^\f\n\r\t\u000B\u0020\u00A0\u2028\u2029].

\w is the same as [0-9A-Z_a-z]. \W is the opposite: [^0-9A-Z_a-z]. This is supposed to represent the characters that appear in words. Unfortunately, the class it defines is useless for working with virtually any real language. If you need to match a class of letters, you must specify your own class.

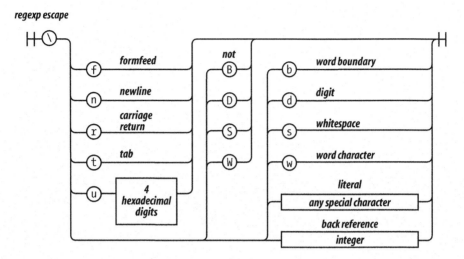

A simple letter class is [A-Za-z\u00C0-\u1FFF\u2800-\uFFFD]. It includes all of Unicode's letters, but it also includes thousands of characters that are not letters. Unicode is large and complex. An exact letter class of the Basic Multilingual Plane is possible, but would be huge and inefficient. JavaScript's regular expressions provide extremely poor support for internationalization.

\b was intended to be a word-boundary anchor that would make it easier to match text on word boundaries. Unfortunately, it uses \w to find word boundaries, so it is completely useless for multilingual applications. This is not a good part.

\1 is a reference to the text that was captured by group 1 so that it can be matched again. For example, you could search text for duplicated words with:

```
var doubled_words =
    /([A-Za-z\u00C0-\u1FFF\u2800-\uFFFD]+)\s+\1/gi;
```

doubled_words looks for occurrences of words (strings containing 1 or more letters) followed by whitespace followed by the same word.

\2 is a reference to group 2, \3 is a reference to group 3, and so on.

## Regexp Group

There are four kinds of groups:

*Capturing*

A capturing group is a regexp choice wrapped in parentheses. The characters that match the group will be captured. Every capture group is given a number. The first capturing ( in the regular expression is group 1. The second capturing ( in the regular expression is group 2.

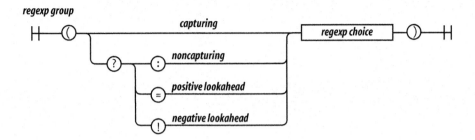

*regexp group*

*Noncapturing*

A noncapturing group has a (?: prefix. A noncapturing group simply matches; it does not capture the matched text. This has the advantage of slight faster performance. Noncapturing groups do not interfere with the numbering of capturing groups.

*Positive lookahead*

A positive lookahead group has a (?= prefix. It is like a noncapturing group except that after the group matches, the text is rewound to where the group started, effectively matching nothing. This is not a good part.

*Negative lookahead*

A negative lookahead group has a (?! prefix. It is like a positive lookahead group, except that it matches only if it fails to match. This is not a good part.

## Regexp Class

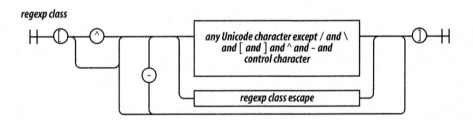

*regexp class*

A *regexp class* is a convenient way of specifying one of a set of characters. For example, if we wanted to match a vowel, we could write (?:a|e|i|o|u), but it is more conveniently written as the class [aeiou].

Classes provide two other conveniences. The first is that ranges of characters can be specified. So, the set of 32 ASCII special characters:

    ! " # $ % & ' ( ) * + , - . / : ; < = > ? @ [ \ ] ^ _ ` { | } ~

could be written as:

    (?:!|"|#|\$|%|&|'|\(|\)|\*|\+|,|-|\.|\/|:|;|<|=|>|@|\[|\\|]|\^|_|`|\{|\||\}|~)

but is slightly more nicely written as:

    [!-\/:-@\[-`{-~]

which includes the characters from ! through / and : through @ and [ through ` and { through ~. It is still pretty nasty looking.

The other convenience is the complementing of a class. If the first character after the [ is ^, then the class excludes the specified characters.

So [^!-\/:-@\[-`{-~] matches any character that is *not* one of the ASCII special characters.

## Regexp Class Escape

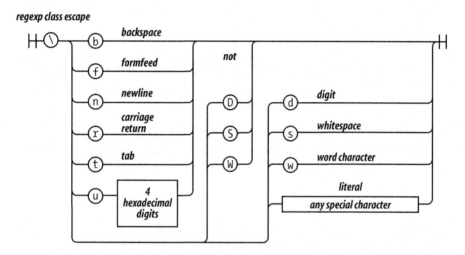

*regexp class escape*

The rules of escapement within a character class are slightly different than those for a regexp factor. [\b] is the backspace character. Here are the special characters that should be escaped in a character class:

    - / [ \ ] ^

## Regexp Quantifier

A *regexp factor* may have a *regexp quantifier* suffix that determines how many times the factor should match. A number wrapped in curly braces means that the factor should match that many times. So, /www/ matches the same as /w{3}/. {3,6} will match 3, 4, 5, or 6 times. {3,} will match 3 or more times.

**regexp quantifier**

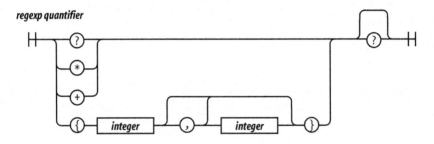

? is the same as {0,1}. * is the same as {0,}. + is the same as {1,}.

Matching tends to be greedy, matching as many repetitions as possible up to the limit, if there is one. If the quantifier has an extra ? suffix, then matching tends to be lazy, attempting to match as few repetitions as possible. It is usually best to stick with the greedy matching.

# CHAPTER 8

# Methods

*Though this be madness, yet there is method in 't.*

—William Shakespeare, *The Tragedy of Hamlet, Prince of Denmark*

JavaScript includes a small set of standard methods that are available on the standard types.

## Array

### *array*.concat(*item...*)

The concat method produces a new array containing a shallow copy of this *array* with the *items* appended to it. If an *item* is an array, then each of its elements is appended individually. Also see *array*.push(*item...*) later in this chapter.

```
var a = ['a', 'b', 'c'];
var b = ['x', 'y', 'z'];
var c = a.concat(b, true);
// c is ['a', 'b', 'c', 'x', 'y', 'z', true]
```

### *array*.join(*separator*)

The join method makes a string from an *array*. It does this by making a string of each of the *array*'s elements, and then concatenating them all together with a *separator* between them. The default *separator* is ','. To join without separation, use an empty string as the *separator*.

If you are assembling a string from a large number of pieces, it is usually faster to put the pieces into an array and join them than it is to concatenate the pieces with the + operator:

```
var a = ['a', 'b', 'c'];
a.push('d');
var c = a.join('');    // c is 'abcd';
```

### array.pop( )

The pop and push methods make an *array* work like a stack. The pop method removes and returns the last element in this *array*. If the *array* is empty, it returns undefined.

```
var a = ['a', 'b', 'c'];
var c = a.pop();    // a is ['a', 'b'] & c is 'c'
```

pop can be implemented like this:

```
Array.method('pop', function () {
    return this.splice(this.length - 1, 1)[0];
});
```

### array.push(*item...*)

The push method appends *items* to the end of an array. Unlike the concat method, it modifies the *array* and appends array items whole. It returns the new length of the *array*:

```
var a = ['a', 'b', 'c'];
var b = ['x', 'y', 'z'];
var c = a.push(b, true);
// a is ['a', 'b', 'c', ['x', 'y', 'z'], true]
// c is 5;
```

push can be implemented like this:

```
Array.method('push', function () {
    this.splice.apply(
        this,
        [this.length, 0].concat(Array.prototype.slice.apply(arguments)));
    return this.length;
});
```

### array.reverse( )

The reverse method modifies the *array* by reversing the order of the elements. It returns the *array*:

```
var a = ['a', 'b', 'c'];
var b = a.reverse();
// both a and b are ['c', 'b', 'a']
```

### array.shift( )

The shift method removes the first element from an *array* and returns it. If the *array* is empty, it returns undefined. shift is usually much slower than pop:

```
var a = ['a', 'b', 'c'];
var c = a.shift();    // a is ['b', 'c'] & c is 'a'
```

shift can be implemented like this:

```
Array.method('shift', function () {
    return this.splice(0, 1)[0];
});
```

### array.slice(*start, end*)

The slice method makes a shallow copy of a portion of an *array*. The first element copied will be *array*[*start*]. It will stop before copying *array*[*end*]. The *end* parameter is optional, and the default is *array*.length. If either parameter is negative, *array*.length will be added to them in an attempt to make them nonnegative. If *start* is greater than or equal to *array*. length, the result will be a new empty array. Do not confuse slice with splice. Also see *string*.slice later in this chapter.

```
var a = ['a', 'b', 'c'];
var b = a.slice(0, 1);    // b is ['a']
var c = a.slice(1);       // c is ['b', 'c']
var d = a.slice(1, 2);    // d is ['b']
```

### array.sort(*comparefn*)

The sort method sorts the contents of an *array* in place. It sorts arrays of numbers incorrectly:

```
var n = [4, 8, 15, 16, 23, 42];
n.sort();
// n is [15, 16, 23, 4, 42, 8]
```

JavaScript's default comparison function assumes that the elements to be sorted are strings. It isn't clever enough to test the type of the elements before comparing them, so it converts the numbers to strings as it compares them, ensuring a shockingly incorrect result.

Fortunately, you may replace the comparison function with your own. Your comparison function should take two parameters and return 0 if the two parameters are equal, a negative number if the first parameter should come first, and a positive number if the second parameter should come first. (Old-timers might be reminded of the FORTRAN II arithmetic IF statement.)

```
n.sort(function (a, b) {
    return a - b;
});
// n is [4, 8, 15, 16, 23, 42];
```

That function will sort numbers, but it doesn't sort strings. If we want to be able to sort any array of simple values, we must work harder:

```
var m = ['aa', 'bb', 'a', 4, 8, 15, 16, 23, 42];
m.sort(function (a, b) {
    if (a === b) {
        return 0;
    }
    if (typeof a === typeof b) {
        return a < b ? -1 : 1;
    }
    return typeof a < typeof b ? -1 : 1;
});
// m is [4, 8, 15, 16, 23, 42, 'a', 'aa', 'bb']
```

If case is not significant, your comparison function should convert the operands to lowercase before comparing them. Also see *string*.localeCompare later in this chapter.

With a smarter comparison function, we can sort an array of objects. To make things easier for the general case, we will write a function that will make comparison functions:

```
    // Function by takes a member name string and returns
    // a comparison function that can be used to sort an
    // array of objects that contain that member.

    var by = function (name) {
        return function (o, p) {
            var a, b;
            if (typeof o === 'object' && typeof p === 'object' && o && p) {
                a = o[name];
                b = p[name];
                if (a === b) {
                    return 0;
                }
                if (typeof a === typeof b) {
                    return a < b ? -1 : 1;
                }
                return typeof a < typeof b ? -1 : 1;
            } else {
                throw {
                    name: 'Error',
                    message: 'Expected an object when sorting by ' + name;
                };
            }
        };
    };

    var s = [
        {first: 'Joe',    last: 'Besser'},
        {first: 'Moe',    last: 'Howard'},
        {first: 'Joe',    last: 'DeRita'},
        {first: 'Shemp', last: 'Howard'},
        {first: 'Larry', last: 'Fine'},
        {first: 'Curly', last: 'Howard'}
    ];
    s.sort(by('first'));    // s is [
    //    {first: 'Curly', last: 'Howard'},
    //    {first: 'Joe',    last: 'DeRita'},
    //    {first: 'Joe',    last: 'Besser'},
    //    {first: 'Larry', last: 'Fine'},
    //    {first: 'Moe',    last: 'Howard'},
    //    {first: 'Shemp', last: 'Howard'}
    // ]
```

The sort method is not stable, so:

```
    s.sort(by('first')).sort(by('last'));
```

is not guaranteed to produce the correct sequence. If you want to sort on multiple keys, you again need to do more work. We can modify by to take a second parameter, another compare method that will be called to break ties when the major key produces a match:

```
    // Function by takes a member name string and an
    // optional minor comparison function and returns
    // a comparison function that can be used to sort an
    // array of objects that contain that member. The
    // minor comparison function is used to break ties
```

```
        // when the o[name] and p[name] are equal.

    var by = function (name, minor) {
        return function (o, p) {
            var a, b;
            if (o && p && typeof o === 'object' && typeof p === 'object') {
                a = o[name];
                b = p[name];
                if (a === b) {
                    return typeof minor === 'function' ? minor(o, p) : 0;
                }
                if (typeof a === typeof b) {
                    return a < b ? -1 : 1;
                }
                return typeof a < typeof b ? -1 : 1;
            } else {
                throw {
                    name: 'Error',
                    message: 'Expected an object when sorting by ' + name;
                };
            }
        };
    };

    s.sort(by('last', by('first')));     // s is [
    //    {first: 'Joe',   last: 'Besser'},
    //    {first: 'Joe',   last: 'DeRita'},
    //    {first: 'Larry', last: 'Fine'},
    //    {first: 'Curly', last: 'Howard'},
    //    {first: 'Moe',   last: 'Howard'},
    //    {first: 'Shemp', last: 'Howard'}
    // ]
```

### array.splice(start, deleteCount, item...)

The splice method removes elements from an *array*, replacing them with new *item*s. The *start* parameter is the number of a position within the *array*. The *deleteCount* parameter is the number of elements to delete starting from that position. If there are additional parameters, those *item*s will be inserted at the position. It returns an array containing the deleted elements.

The most popular use of splice is to delete elements from an array. Do not confuse splice with slice:

```
    var a = ['a', 'b', 'c'];
    var r = a.splice(1, 1, 'ache', 'bug');
    // a is ['a', 'ache', 'bug', 'c']
    // r is ['b']
```

splice can be implemented like this:

```
    Array.method('splice', function (start, deleteCount) {
        var max = Math.max,
            min = Math.min,
            delta,
            element,
```

```
                insertCount = max(arguments.length - 2, 0),
                k = 0,
                len = this.length,
                new_len,
                result = [],
                shift_count;

        start = start || 0;
        if (start < 0) {
            start += len;
        }
        start = max(min(start, len), 0);
        deleteCount = max(min(typeof deleteCount === 'number' ?
                deleteCount : len, len - start), 0);
        delta = insertCount - deleteCount;
        new_len = len + delta;
        while (k < deleteCount) {
            element = this[start + k];
            if (element !== undefined) {
                result[k] = element;
            }
            k += 1;
        }
        shift_count = len - start - deleteCount;
        if (delta < 0) {
            k = start + insertCount;
            while (shift_count) {
                this[k] = this[k - delta];
                k += 1;
                shift_count -= 1;
            }
            this.length = new_len;
        } else if (delta > 0) {
            k = 1;
            while (shift_count) {
                this[new_len - k] = this[len - k];
                k += 1;
                shift_count -= 1;
            }
            this.length = new_len;
        }
        for (k = 0; k < insertCount; k += 1) {
            this[start + k] = arguments[k + 2];
        }
        return result;
    });
```

### array.unshift(item...)

The unshift method is like the push method except that it shoves the *item*s onto the front of this *array* instead of at the end. It returns the *array*'s new length:

```
var a = ['a', 'b', 'c'];
var r = a.unshift('?', '@');
// a is ['?', '@', 'a', 'b', 'c']
// r is 5
```

unshift can be implemented like this:

```
Array.method('unshift', function () {
    this.splice.apply(this,
        [0, 0].concat(Array.prototype.slice.apply(arguments)));
    return this.length;
});
```

## Function

### *function*.apply(*thisArg, argArray*)

The apply method invokes a *function*, passing in the object that will be bound to this and an optional array of arguments. The apply method is used in the apply invocation pattern (Chapter 4):

```
Function.method('bind', function (that) {

// Return a function that will call this function as
// though it is a method of that object.

    var method = this,
        slice = Array.prototype.slice,
        args = slice.apply(arguments, [1]);
    return function () {
        return method.apply(that,
            args.concat(slice.apply(arguments, [0])));
    };
});

var x = function () {
    return this.value;
}.bind({value: 666});
alert(x());  // 666
```

## Number

### *number*.toExponential(*fractionDigits*)

The toExponential method converts this *number* to a string in the exponential form. The optional *fractionDigits* parameter controls the number of decimal places. It should be between 0 and 20:

```
document.writeln(Math.PI.toExponential(0));
document.writeln(Math.PI.toExponential(2));
document.writeln(Math.PI.toExponential(7));
document.writeln(Math.PI.toExponential(16));
document.writeln(Math.PI.toExponential());

// Produces
```

```
3e+0
3.14e+0
3.1415927e+0
3.1415926535897930e+0
3.141592653589793e+0
```

### number.toFixed(*fractionDigits*)

The toFixed method converts this *number* to a string in the decimal form. The optional *fractionDigits* parameter controls the number of decimal places. It should be between 0 and 20. The default is 0:

```
document.writeln(Math.PI.toFixed(0));
document.writeln(Math.PI.toFixed(2));
document.writeln(Math.PI.toFixed(7));
document.writeln(Math.PI.toFixed(16));
document.writeln(Math.PI.toFixed( ));

// Produces

3
3.14
3.1415927
3.1415926535897930
3
```

### number.toPrecision(*precision*)

The toPrecision method converts this *number* to a string in the decimal form. The optional *precision* parameter controls the number of digits of precision. It should be between 1 and 21:

```
document.writeln(Math.PI.toPrecision(2));
document.writeln(Math.PI.toPrecision(7));
document.writeln(Math.PI.toPrecision(16));
document.writeln(Math.PI.toPrecision( ));

// Produces

3.1
3.141593
3.141592653589793
3.141592653589793
```

### number.toString(*radix*)

The toString method converts this *number* to a string. The optional *radix* parameter controls radix, or base. It should be between 2 and 36. The default *radix* is base 10. The *radix* parameter is most commonly used with integers, but it can be used on any number.

The most common case, *number*.toString( ), can be written more simply as String(*number*):

```
document.writeln(Math.PI.toString(2));
document.writeln(Math.PI.toString(8));
document.writeln(Math.PI.toString(16));
document.writeln(Math.PI.toString( ));
```

```
// Produces

11.00100100001111110110101010001000100001011010100011
3.1103755242102643
3.243f6a8885a3
3.141592653589793
```

# Object

### *object*.hasOwnProperty(*name*)

The hasOwnProperty method returns true if the *object* contains a property having the *name*. The prototype chain is not examined. This method is useless if the *name* is hasOwnProperty:

```
var a = {member: true};
var b = Object.create(a);          // from Chapter 3
var t = a.hasOwnProperty('member');  // t is true
var u = b.hasOwnProperty('member');  // u is false
var v = b.member;                  // v is true
```

# RegExp

### *regexp*.exec(*string*)

The exec method is the most powerful (and slowest) of the methods that use regular expressions. If it successfully matches the *regexp* and the *string*, it returns an array. The 0 element of the array will contain the substring that matched the *regexp*. The 1 element is the text captured by group 1, the 2 element is the text captured by group 2, and so on. If the match fails, it returns null.

If the *regexp* has a g flag, things are a little more complicated. The searching begins not at position 0 of the string, but at position *regexp*.lastIndex (which is initially zero). If the match is successful, then *regexp*.lastIndex will be set to the position of the first character after the match. An unsuccessful match resets *regexp*.lastIndex to 0.

This allows you to search for several occurrences of a pattern in a string by calling exec in a loop. There are a couple things to watch out for. If you exit the loop early, you must reset *regexp*.lastIndex to 0 yourself before entering the loop again. Also, the ^ factor matches only when *regexp*.lastIndex is 0:

```
// Break a simple html text into tags and texts.
// (See string.replace for the entityify method.)

// For each tag or text, produce an array containing
// [0] The full matched tag or text
// [1] The /, if there is one
// [2] The tag name
// [3] The attributes, if any

var text = '<html><body bgcolor=linen><p>' +
        'This is <b>bold<\/b>!<\/p><\/body><\/html>';
```

```
var tags = /[^<>]+|<(\/?)([A-Za-z]+)([^<>]*)>/g;
var a, i;

while ((a = tags.exec(text))) {
    for (i = 0; i < a.length; i += 1) {
        document.writeln(('// [' + i + '] ' + a[i]).entityify());
    }
    document.writeln();
}

// Result:

// [0] <html>
// [1]
// [2] html
// [3]

// [0] <body bgcolor=linen>
// [1]
// [2] body
// [3]  bgcolor=linen

// [0] <p>
// [1]
// [2] p
// [3]

// [0] This is
// [1] undefined
// [2] undefined
// [3] undefined

// [0] <b>
// [1]
// [2] b
// [3]

// [0] bold
// [1] undefined
// [2] undefined
// [3] undefined

// [0] </b>
// [1] /
// [2] b
// [3]

// [0] !
// [1] undefined
// [2] undefined
// [3] undefined

// [0] </p>
// [1] /
// [2] p
// [3]

// [0] </body>
```

```
// [1] /
// [2] body
// [3]

// [0] </html>
// [1] /
// [2] html
// [3]
```

### regexp.test(string)

The test method is the simplest (and fastest) of the methods that use regular expressions. If the *regexp* matches the *string*, it returns true; otherwise, it returns false. Do not use the g flag with this method:

```
var b = /&.+;/.test('frank &amp; beans');
// b is true
```

test could be implemented as:

```
RegExp.method('test', function (string) {
    return this.exec(string) !== null;
});
```

---

## String

### string.charAt(pos)

The charAt method returns the character at position *pos* in this *string*. If *pos* is less than zero or greater than or equal to *string*.length, it returns the empty string. JavaScript does not have a character type. The result of this method is a string:

```
var name = 'Curly';
var initial = name.charAt(0);     // initial is 'C'
```

charAt could be implemented as:

```
String.method('charAt', function (pos) {
    return this.slice(pos, pos + 1);
});
```

### string.charCodeAt(pos)

The charCodeAt method is the same as charAt except that instead of returning a string, it returns an integer representation of the code point value of the character at position *pos* in that *string*. If *pos* is less than zero or greater than or equal to *string*.length, it returns NaN:

```
var name = 'Curly';
var initial = name.charCodeAt(0);     // initial is 67
```

### string.concat(string...)

The concat method makes a new string by concatenating other strings together. It is rarely used because the + operator is more convenient:

```
var s = 'C'.concat('a', 't');     // s is 'Cat'
```

### string.indexOf(searchString, position)

The indexOf method searches for a *searchString* within a *string*. If it is found, it returns the position of the first matched character; otherwise, it returns −1. The optional *position* parameter causes the search to begin at some specified position in the *string*:

```
var text = 'Mississippi';
var p = text.indexOf('ss');      // p is 2
p = text.indexOf('ss', 3);       // p is 5
p = text.indexOf('ss', 6);       // p is -1
```

### *string*.**lastIndexOf**(*searchString, position*)

The lastIndexOf method is like the indexOf method, except that it searches from the end of the string instead of the front:

```
var text = 'Mississippi';
var p = text.lastIndexOf('ss');     // p is 5
p = text.lastIndexOf('ss', 3);      // p is 2
p = text.lastIndexOf('ss', 6);      // p is 5
```

### *string*.**localeCompare**(*that*)

The localeCompare method compares two strings. The rules for how the strings are compared are not specified. If this *string* is less than *that* string, the result is negative. If they are equal, the result is zero. This is similar to the convention for the *array*.sort comparison function:

```
var m = ['AAA', 'A', 'aa', 'a', 'Aa', 'aaa'];
m.sort(function (a, b) {
    return a.localeCompare(b);
});
// m (in some locale) is
//      ['a', 'A', 'aa', 'Aa', 'aaa', 'AAA']
```

### *string*.**match**(*regexp*)

The match method matches a string and a regular expression. How it does this depends on the g flag. If there is no g flag, then the result of calling *string*.match(*regexp*) is the same as calling *regexp*.exec(*string*). However, if the *regexp* has the g flag, then it produces an array of all the matches but excludes the capturing groups:

```
var text = '<html><body bgcolor=linen><p>' +
        'This is <b>bold<\/b>!<\/p><\/body><\/html>';
var tags = /[^<>]+|<(\/?)([A-Za-z]+)([^<>]*)>/g;
var a, i;

a = text.match(tags);
for (i = 0; i < a.length; i += 1) {
    document.writeln(('// [' + i + '] ' + a[i]).entityify());
}

// The result is

// [0] <html>
// [1] <body bgcolor=linen>
// [2] <p>
// [3] This is
// [4] <b>
// [5] bold
// [6] </b>
// [7] !
```

```
// [8] </p>
// [9] </body>
// [10] </html>
```

### string.replace(searchValue, replaceValue)

The replace method does a search and replace operation on this *string*, producing a new string. The *searchValue* argument can be a string or a regular expression object. If it is a string, *only* the first occurrence of the *searchValue* is replaced, so:

```
var result = "mother_in_law".replace('_', '-');
```

will produce "mother-in_law", which might be a disappointment.

If *searchValue* is a regular expression and if it has the g flag, then it will replace all occurrences. If it does not have the g flag, then it will replace only the first occurrence.

The *replaceValue* can be a string or a function. If *replaceValue* is a string, the character $ has special meaning:

```
// Capture 3 digits within parens

var oldareacode = /\((\d{3})\)/g;
var p = '(555)666-1212'.replace(oldareacode, '$1-');
// p is '555-666-1212'
```

| Dollar sequence | Replacement |
| --- | --- |
| $$ | $ |
| $& | The matched text |
| $*number* | Capture group text |
| $` | The text preceding the match |
| $' | The text following the match |

If the *replaceValue* is a function, it will be called for each match, and the string returned by the function will be used as the replacement text. The first parameter passed to the function is the matched text. The second parameter is the text of capture group 1, the next parameter is the text of capture group 2, and so on:

```
String.method('entityify', function () {

    var character = {
        '<' : '&lt;',
        '>' : '&gt;',
        '&' : '&amp;',
        '"' : '&quot;'
    };

// Return the string.entityify method, which
// returns the result of calling the replace method.
// Its replaceValue function returns the result of
// looking a character up in an object. This use of
// an object usually outperforms switch statements.
```

```
        return function () {
            return this.replace(/[<>&"]/g, function (c) {
                return character[c];
            });
        };
    }());
alert("<&>".entityify());   // &lt;&amp;&gt;
```

### string.search(regexp)

The search method is like the indexOf method, except that it takes a regular expression object instead of a string. It returns the position of the first character of the first match, if there is one, or −1 if the search fails. The g flag is ignored. There is no *position* parameter:

```
var text = 'and in it he says "Any damn fool could';
var pos = text.search(/["']/);    // pos is 18
```

### string.slice(start, end)

The slice method makes a new string by copying a portion of another *string*. If the *start* parameter is negative, it adds string.length to it. The *end* parameter is optional, and its default value is string.length. If the *end* parameter is negative, then string.length is added to it. The *end* parameter is one greater than the position of the last character. To get n characters starting at position p, use string.slice(p, p + n). Also see string.substring and array.slice, later and earlier in this chapter, respectively.

```
var text = 'and in it he says "Any damn fool could';
var a = text.slice(18);
// a is '"Any damn fool could'
var b = text.slice(0, 3);
// b is 'and'
var c = text.slice(-5);
// c is 'could'
var d = text.slice(19, 32);
// d is 'Any damn fool'
```

### string.split(separator, limit)

The split method creates an array of strings by splitting this *string* into pieces. The optional *limit* parameter can limit the number of pieces that will be split. The *separator* parameter can be a string or a regular expression.

If the *separator* is the empty string, an array of single characters is produced:

```
var digits = '0123456789';
var a = digits.split('', 5);
// a is ['0', '1', '2', '3', '4']
```

Otherwise, the *string* is searched for all occurrences of the *separator*. Each unit of text between the separators is copied into the array. The g flag is ignored:

```
var ip = '192.168.1.0';
var b = ip.split('.');
// b is ['192', '168', '1', '0']

var c = '|a|b|c|'.split('|');
// c is ['', 'a', 'b', 'c', '']
```

```
var text = 'last,  first  ,middle';
var d = text.split(/\s*,\s*/);
// d is [
//    'last',
//    'first',
//    'middle'
// ]
```

There are some special cases to watch out for. Text from capturing groups will be included in the split:

```
var e = text.split(/\s*(,)\s*/);
// e is [
//    'last',
//    ',',
//    'first',
//    ',',
//    'middle'
// ]
```

Some implementations suppress empty strings in the output array when the *separator* is a regular expression:

```
var f = '|a|b|c|'.split(/\|/);
// f is ['a', 'b', 'c'] on some systems, and
// f is ['', 'a', 'b', 'c', ''] on others
```

### *string*.substring(*start, end*)

The substring method is the same as the slice method except that it doesn't handle the adjustment for negative parameters. There is no reason to use the substring method. Use slice instead.

### *string*.toLocaleLowerCase( )

The toLocaleLowerCase method produces a new string that is made by converting this *string* to lowercase using the rules for the locale. This is primarily for the benefit of Turkish because in that language 'I' converts to ı, not 'i'.

### *string*.toLocaleUpperCase( )

The toLocaleUpperCase method produces a new string that is made by converting this *string* to uppercase using the rules for the locale. This is primarily for the benefit of Turkish, because in that language 'i' converts to 'İ', not 'I'.

### *string*.toLowerCase( )

The toLowerCase method produces a new string that is made by converting this *string* to lowercase.

### *string*.toUpperCase( )

The toUpperCase method produces a new string that is made by converting this *string* to uppercase.

### String.fromCharCode(*char...*)

The String.fromCharCode function produces a string from a series of numbers.

```
var a = String.fromCharCode(67, 97, 116);
// a is 'Cat'
```

# CHAPTER 9

# Style

*Here is a silly stately style indeed!*
—William Shakespeare, *The First Part of Henry the Sixth*

Computer programs are the most complex things that humans make. Programs are made up of a huge number of parts, expressed as functions, statements, and expressions that are arranged in sequences that must be virtually free of error. The runtime behavior has little resemblance to the program that implements it. Software is usually expected to be modified over the course of its productive life. The process of converting one correct program into a different correct program is extremely challenging.

Good programs have a structure that anticipates—but is not overly burdened by— the possible modifications that will be required in the future. Good programs also have a clear presentation. If a program is expressed well, then we have the best chance of being able to understand it so that it can be successfully modified or repaired.

These concerns are true for all programming languages, and are especially true for JavaScript. JavaScript's loose typing and excessive error tolerance provide little compile-time assurance of our programs' quality, so to compensate, we should code with strict discipline.

JavaScript contains a large set of weak or problematic features that can undermine our attempts to write good programs. We should obviously avoid JavaScript's worst features. Surprisingly, perhaps, we should also avoid the features that are often useful but occasionally hazardous. Such features are attractive nuisances, and by avoiding them, a large class of potential errors is avoided.

The long-term value of software to an organization is in direct proportion to the quality of the codebase. Over its lifetime, a program will be handled by many pairs of hands and eyes. If a program is able to clearly communicate its structure and characteristics, it is less likely to break when it is modified in the never-too-distant future.

JavaScript code is often sent directly to the public. It should always be of publication quality. Neatness counts. By writing in a clear and consistent style, your programs become easier to read.

Programmers can debate endlessly on what constitutes good style. Most programmers are firmly rooted in what they're used to, such as the prevailing style where they went to school, or at their first job. Some have had profitable careers with no sense of style at all. Isn't that proof that style doesn't matter? And even if style doesn't matter, isn't one style as good as any other?

It turns out that style matters in programming for the same reason that it matters in writing. It makes for better reading.

Computer programs are sometimes thought of as a write-only medium, so it matters little how it is written as long as it works. But it turns out that the likelihood a program will work is significantly enhanced by our ability to read it, which also increases the likelihood that it actually works as intended. It is also the nature of software to be extensively modified over its productive life. If we can read and understand it, then we can hope to modify and improve it.

Throughout this book I have used a consistent style. My intention was to make the code examples as easy to read as possible. I used whitespace consistently to give you more cues about the meaning of my programs.

I indented the contents of blocks and object literals four spaces. I placed a space between if and ( so that the if didn't look like a function invocation. Only in invocations do I make ( adjacent with the preceding symbol. I put spaces around all infix operators except for . and [, which do not get spaces because they have higher precedence. I use a space after every comma and colon.

I put at most one statement on a line. Multiple statements on a line can be misread. If a statement doesn't fit on a line, I will break it after a comma or a binary operator. That gives more protection against copy/paste errors that are masked by semicolon insertion. (The tragedy of semicolon insertion will be revealed in Appendix A.) I indent the remainder of the statement an extra four spaces, or eight spaces if four would be ambiguous (such as a line break in the condition part of an if statement).

I *always* use blocks with structured statements such as if and while because it is less error prone. I have seen:

```
if (a)
    b( );
```

become:

```
if (a)
    b( );
    c( );
```

which is an error that is very difficult to spot. It looks like:

```
if (a) {
    b( );
    c( );
}
```

but it means:

```
if (a) {
    b( );
}
c( );
```

Code that appears to mean one thing but actually means another is likely to cause bugs. A pair of braces is really cheap protection against bugs that can be expensive to find.

I always use the K&R style, putting the { at the end of a line instead of the front, because it avoids a horrible design blunder in JavaScript's return statement.

I included some comments. I like to put comments in my programs to leave information that will be read at a later time by people (possibly myself) who will need to understand what I was thinking. Sometimes I think about comments as a time machine that I use to send important messages to future me.

I struggle to keep comments up-to-date. Erroneous comments can make programs even harder to read and understand. I can't afford that.

I tried to not waste your time with useless comments like this:

```
i = 0; // Set i to zero.
```

In JavaScript, I prefer to use line comments. I reserve block comments for formal documentation and for commenting out.

I prefer to make the structure of my programs self-illuminating, eliminating the need for comments. I am not always successful, so while my programs are awaiting perfection, I am writing comments.

JavaScript has C syntax, but its blocks don't have scope. So, the convention that variables should be declared at their first use is really bad advice in JavaScript. JavaScript has function scope, but not block scope, so I declare all of my variables at the beginning of each function. JavaScript allows variables to be declared after they are used. That feels like a mistake to me, and I don't want to write programs that look like mistakes. I want my mistakes to stand out. Similarly, I never use an assignment expression in the condition part of an if because:

```
if (a = b) { ... }
```

is probably intended to be:

```
if (a === b) { ... }
```

I want to avoid idioms that look like mistakes.

I never allow switch cases to fall through to the next case. I once found a bug in my code caused by an unintended fall through immediately after having made a vigorous speech about why fall through was sometimes useful. I was fortunate in that I was able to learn from the experience. When reviewing the features of a language, I now pay special attention to features that are sometimes useful but occasionally dangerous. Those are the *worst parts* because it is difficult to tell whether they are being used correctly. That is a place where bugs hide.

Quality was not a motivating concern in the design, implementation, or standardization of JavaScript. That puts a greater burden on the users of the language to resist the language's weaknesses.

JavaScript provides support for large programs, but it also provides forms and idioms that work against large programs. For example, JavaScript provides conveniences for the use of global variables, but global variables become increasingly problematic as programs scale in complexity.

I use a single global variable to contain an application or library. Every object has its own namespace, so it is easy to use objects to organize my code. Use of closure provides further information hiding, increasing the strength of my modules.

# CHAPTER 10
# Beautiful Features

*Thus, expecting thy reply, I profane my lips on thy*
*foot, my eyes on thy picture, and my heart on thy*
*every part. Thine, in the dearest design of industry…*
—William Shakespeare, *Love's Labor's Lost*

I was invited last year to contribute a chapter to Andy Oram's and Greg Wilson's *Beautiful Code* (O'Reilly), an anthology on the theme of beauty as expressed in computer programs. I wanted to write my chapter in JavaScript. I wanted to use it to present something abstract, powerful, and useful to show that the language was up to it. And I wanted to avoid the browser and other venues in which JavaScript is typecast. I wanted to show something respectable with some heft to it.

I immediately thought of Vaughn Pratt's Top Down Operator Precedence parser, which I use in JSLint (see Appendix C). Parsing is an important topic in computing. The ability to write a compiler for a language in itself is still a test for the completeness of a language.

I wanted to include all of the code for a parser in JavaScript that parses JavaScript. But my chapter was just one of 30 or 40, so I felt constrained in the number of pages I could consume. A further complication was that most of my readers would have no experience with JavaScript, so I also would have to introduce the language and its peculiarities.

So, I decided to subset the language. That way, I wouldn't have to parse the whole language, and I wouldn't have to describe the whole language. I called the subset Simplified JavaScript. Selecting the subset was easy: it included just the features that I needed to write a parser. This is how I described it in *Beautiful Code*:

> Simplified JavaScript is just the good stuff, including:
>
> *Functions as first class objects*
> Functions in Simplified JavaScript are lambdas with lexical scoping.

*Dynamic objects with prototypal inheritance*
> Objects are class-free. We can add a new member to any object by ordinary assignment. An object can inherit members from another object.

*Object literals and array literals*
> This is a very convenient notation for creating new objects and arrays. JavaScript literals were the inspiration for the JSON data interchange format.

The subset contained the best of the Good Parts. Even though it was a small language, it was very expressive and powerful. JavaScript has lots of additional features that really don't add very much, and as you'll find in the appendixes that follow, it has a lot of features with negative value. There was nothing ugly or bad in the subset. All of that fell away.

Simplified JavaScript isn't strictly a subset. I added a few new features. The simplest was adding pi as a simple constant. I did that to demonstrate a feature of the parser. I also demonstrated a better reserved word policy and showed that reserved words are unnecessary. In a function, a word cannot be used as both a variable or parameter name and a language feature. You can use a word for one or the other, and the programmer gets to choose. That makes a language easier to learn because you don't need to be aware of features you don't use. And it makes the language easier to extend because it isn't necessary to reserve more words to add new features.

I also added block scope. Block scope is not a necessary feature, but not having it confuses experienced programmers. I included block scope because I anticipated that my parser would be used to parse languages that are not JavaScript, and those languages would do scoping correctly. The code I wrote for the parser is written in a style that doesn't care if block scope is available or not. I recommend that you write that way, too.

When I started thinking about this book, I wanted to take the subset idea further, to show how to take an existing programming language and make significant improvements to it by making no changes except to exclude the low-value features.

We see a lot of feature-driven product design in which the cost of features is not properly accounted. Features can have a negative value to consumers because they make the products more difficult to understand and use. We are finding that people like products that just work. It turns out that designs that just work are much harder to produce than designs that assemble long lists of features.

Features have a specification cost, a design cost, and a development cost. There is a testing cost and a reliability cost. The more features there are, the more likely one will develop problems or will interact badly with another. In software systems, there is a storage cost, which was becoming negligible, but in mobile applications is becoming significant again. There are ascending performance costs because Moore's Law doesn't apply to batteries.

Features have a documentation cost. Every feature adds pages to the manual, increasing training costs. Features that offer value to a minority of users impose a cost on all users. So, in designing products and programming languages, we want to get the core features—the good parts—right because that is where we create most of the value.

We all find the good parts in the products that we use. We value simplicity, and when simplicity isn't offered to us, we make it ourselves. My microwave oven has tons of features, but the only ones I use are cook and the clock. And setting the clock is a struggle. We cope with the complexity of feature-driven design by finding and sticking with the good parts.

It would be nice if products and programming languages were designed to have only good parts.

# Awful Parts

*That will prove awful both in deed and word.*
—William Shakespeare, *Pericles, Prince of Tyre*

In this appendix, I present the problematic features of JavaScript that are not easily avoided. You must be aware of these things and be prepared to cope.

## Global Variables

The worst of all of JavaScript's bad features is its dependence on global variables. A *global variable* is a variable that is visible in every scope. Global variables can be a convenience in very small programs, but they quickly become unwieldy as programs get larger. Because a global variable can be changed by any part of the program at any time, they can significantly complicate the behavior of the program. Use of global variables degrades the reliability of the programs that use them.

Global variables make it harder to run independent subprograms in the same program. If the subprograms happen to have global variables that share the same names, then they will interfere with each other and likely fail, usually in difficult to diagnose ways.

Lots of languages have global variables. For example, Java's public static members are global variables. The problem with JavaScript isn't just that it allows them, it requires them. JavaScript does not have a linker. All compilation units are loaded into a common global object.

There are three ways to define global variables. The first is to place a var statement outside of any function:

```
var foo = value;
```

The second is to add a property directly to the global object. The global object is the container of all global variables. In web browsers, the global object goes by the name window:

```
window.foo = value;
```

The third is to use a variable without declaring it. This is called *implied global*:

```
foo = value;
```

This was intended as a convenience to beginners by making it unnecessary to declare variables before using them. Unfortunately, forgetting to declare a variable is a very common mistake. JavaScript's policy of making forgotten variables global creates bugs that can be very difficult to find.

# Scope

JavaScript's syntax comes from C. In all other C-like languages, a block (a set of statements wrapped in curly braces) creates a scope. Variables declared in a block are not visible outside of the block. JavaScript uses the block syntax, but does not provide block scope: a variable declared in a block is visible everywhere in the function containing the block. This can be surprising to programmers with experience in other languages.

In most languages, it is generally best to declare variables at the site of first use. That turns out to be a bad practice in JavaScript because it does not have block scope. It is better to declare all variables at the top of each function.

# Semicolon Insertion

JavaScript has a mechanism that tries to correct faulty programs by automatically inserting semicolons. Do not depend on this. It can mask more serious errors.

It sometimes inserts semicolons in places where they are not welcome. Consider the consequences of semicolon insertion on the return statement. If a return statement returns a value, that value expression must begin on the same line as the return:

```
return
{
    status: true
};
```

This appears to return an object containing a status member. Unfortunately, semicolon insertion turns it into a statement that returns undefined. There is no warning that semicolon insertion caused the misinterpretation of the program. The problem can be avoided if the { is placed at the end of the previous line and not at the beginning of the next line:

```
return {
    status: true
};
```

# Reserved Words

The following words are reserved in JavaScript:

```
abstract boolean break byte case catch char class const continue debugger default
delete do double else enum export extends false final finally float for function goto
if implements import in instanceof int interface long native new null package private
protected public return short static super switch synchronized this throw throws
transient true try typeof var volatile void while with
```

Most of these words are not used in the language.

They cannot be used to name variables or parameters. When reserved words are used as keys in object literals, they must be quoted. They cannot be used with the dot notation, so it is sometimes necessary to use the bracket notation instead:

```
var method;                // ok
var class;                 // illegal
object = {box: value};     // ok
object = {case: value};    // illegal
object = {'case': value};  // ok
object.box = value;        // ok
object.case = value;       // illegal
object['case'] = value;    // ok
```

# Unicode

JavaScript was designed at a time when Unicode was expected to have at most 65,536 characters. It has since grown to have a capacity of more than 1 million characters.

JavaScript's characters are 16 bits. That is enough to cover the original 65,536 (which is now known as the Basic Multilingual Plane). Each of the remaining million characters can be represented as a pair of characters. Unicode considers the pair to be a single character. JavaScript thinks the pair is two distinct characters.

# typeof

The typeof operator returns a string that identifies the type of its operand. So:

```
typeof 98.6
```

produces 'number'. Unfortunately:

```
typeof null
```

returns 'object' instead of 'null'. Oops. A better test for null is simply:

```
my_value === null
```

A bigger problem is testing a value for objectness. typeof cannot distinguish between null and objects, but you can because null is falsy and all objects are truthy:

```
if (my_value && typeof my_value === 'object') {
    // my_value is an object or an array!
}
```

Also see the later sections "NaN" and "Phony Arrays."

Implementations disagree on the type of regular expression objects. Some implementations report that:

```
typeof /a/
```

is 'object', and others say that it is 'function'. It might have been more useful to report 'regexp', but the standard does not allow that.

## parseInt

parseInt is a function that converts a string into an integer. It stops when it sees a nondigit, so parseInt("16") and parseInt("16 tons") produce the same result. It would be nice if the function somehow informed us about the extra text, but it doesn't.

If the first character of the string is 0, then the string is evaluated in base 8 instead of base 10. In base 8, 8 and 9 are not digits, so parseInt("08") and parseInt("09") produce 0 as their result. This error causes problems in programs that parse dates and times. Fortunately, parseInt can take a radix parameter, so that parseInt("08", 10) produces 8. I recommend that you always provide the radix parameter.

## +

The + operator can add or concatenate. Which one it does depends on the types of the parameters. If either operand is an empty string, it produces the other operand converted to a string. If both operands are numbers, it produces the sum. Otherwise, it converts both operands to strings and concatenates them. This complicated behavior is a common source of bugs. If you intend + to add, make sure that both operands are numbers.

## Floating Point

Binary floating-point numbers are inept at handling decimal fractions, so 0.1 + 0.2 is not equal to 0.3. This is the most frequently reported bug in JavaScript, and it is an intentional consequence of having adopted the IEEE Standard for Binary Floating-Point Arithmetic (IEEE 754). This standard is well-suited for many applications, but it violates most of the things you learned about numbers in middle school.

Fortunately, integer arithmetic in floating point is exact, so decimal representation errors can be avoided by scaling.

For example, dollar values can be converted to whole cents values by multiplying them by 100. The cents then can be accurately added. The sum can be divided by 100 to convert back into dollars. People have a reasonable expectation when they count money that the results will be exact.

# NaN

The value NaN is a special quantity defined by IEEE 754. It stands for *not a number*, even though:

```
typeof NaN === 'number'    // true
```

The value can be produced by attempting to convert a string to a number when the string is not in the form of a number. For example:

```
+ '0'      // 0
+ 'oops'   // NaN
```

If NaN is an operand in an arithmetic operation, then NaN will be the result. So, if you have a chain of formulas that produce NaN as a result, at least one of the inputs was NaN, or NaN was generated somewhere.

You can test for NaN. As we have seen, typeof does not distinguish between numbers and NaN, and it turns out that NaN is not equal to itself. So, surprisingly:

```
NaN === NaN    // false
NaN !== NaN    // true
```

JavaScript provides an isNaN function that can distinguish between numbers and NaN:

```
isNaN(NaN)       // true
isNaN(0)         // false
isNaN('oops')    // true
isNaN('0')       // false
```

The isFinite function is the best way of determining whether a value can be used as a number because it rejects NaN and Infinity. Unfortunately, isFinite will attempt to convert its operand to a number, so it is not a good test if a value is not actually a number. You may want to define your own isNumber function:

```
var isNumber = function isNumber(value) { return typeof value === 'number' &&
        isFinite(value);
}
```

# Phony Arrays

JavaScript does not have real arrays. That isn't all bad. JavaScript's arrays are really easy to use. There is no need to give them a dimension, and they never generate out-of-bounds errors. But their performance can be considerably worse than real arrays.

The typeof operator does not distinguish between arrays and objects. To determine that a value is an array, you also need to consult its constructor property:

```
if (my_value && typeof my_value === 'object' &&
        my_value.constructor === Array) {
    // my_value is an array!
}
```

That test will give a false negative if an array was created in a different frame or window. This test is more reliable when the value might have been created in another frame:

```
if (Object.prototype.toString.apply(my_value) === '[object Array]'){
    // my_value is truly an array!
}
```

The arguments array is not an array; it is an object with a `length` member. These tests will not identify the arguments array as an array.

## Falsy Values

JavaScript has a surprisingly large set of falsy values, shown in Table A-1.

*Table A-1. The many falsy values of JavaScript*

| Value | Type |
|-------|------|
| 0 | Number |
| NaN (not a number) | Number |
| ' ' (empty string) | String |
| false | Boolean |
| null | Object |
| undefined | Undefined |

These values are all falsy, but they are not interchangeable. For example, this is the wrong way to determine if an object is missing a member:

```
value = myObject[name];
if (value == null) {
    alert(name + ' not found.');
}
```

undefined is the value of missing members, but the snippet is testing for null. It is using the == operator (see Appendix B), which does type coercion, instead of the more reliable === operator. Sometimes those two errors cancel each other out. Sometimes they don't.

undefined and NaN are not constants. They are global variables, and you can change their values. That should not be possible, and yet it is. Don't do it.

## hasOwnProperty

In Chapter 3, the hasOwnProperty method was offered as a filter to work around a problem with the for in statement. Unfortunately, hasOwnProperty is a method, not an operator, so in any object it could be replaced with a different function or even a value that is not a function:

```
var name;
another_stooge.hasOwnProperty = null;        // trouble
for (name in another_stooge) {
    if (another_stooge.hasOwnProperty(name)) { // boom
        document.writeln(name + ': ' + another_stooge[name]);
    }
}
```

## Object

JavaScript's objects are never truly empty because they can pick up members from the prototype chain. Sometimes that matters. For example, suppose you are writing a program that counts the number of occurrences of each word in a text. We can use the toLowerCase method to normalize the text to lowercase, and then use the split method with a regular expression to produce an array of words. We can then loop through the words and count the number of times we see each one:

```
var i;
var word;
var text =
        "This oracle of comfort has so pleased me, " +
        "That when I am in heaven I shall desire " +
        "To see what this child does, " +
        "and praise my Constructor.";

var words = text.toLowerCase().split(/[\s,.]+/);
var count = {};
for (i = 0; i < words.length; i += 1) {
    word = words[i];
    if (count[word]) {
        count[word] += 1;
    } else {
        count[word] = 1;
    }
}
```

If we look at the results, count['this'] is 2 and count.heaven is 1, but count. constructor contains a crazy looking string. The reason is that the count object inherits from Object.prototype, and Object.prototype contains a member named constructor whose value is Object. The += operator, like the + operator, does concatenation rather than addition when its operands are not numbers. Object is a function, so += converts it to a string somehow and concatenates a 1 to its butt.

We can avoid problems like this the same way we avoid problems with for in: by testing for membership with the hasOwnProperty method or by looking for specific types. In this case, our test for the truthiness of count[word] was not specific enough. We could have written instead:

```
if (typeof count[word] === 'number') {
```

# Bad Parts

*And, I pray thee now, tell me for*
*which of my bad parts didst thou first fall in love with me?*
—William Shakespeare, *Much Ado About Nothing*

In this appendix, I present some of the problematic features of JavaScript that are easily avoided. By simply avoiding these features, you make JavaScript a better language, and yourself a better programmer.

## ==

JavaScript has two sets of equality operators: `===` and `!==`, and their evil twins `==` and `!=`. The good ones work the way you would expect. If the two operands are of the same type and have the same value, then `===` produces `true` and `!==` produces `false`. The evil twins do the right thing when the operands are of the same type, but if they are of different types, they attempt to coerce the values. The rules by which they do that are complicated and unmemorable. These are some of the interesting cases:

```
''  == '0'          // false
0 == ''             // true
0 == '0'            // true

false == 'false'    // false
false == '0'        // true

false == undefined  // false
false == null       // false
null == undefined   // true

' \t\r\n ' == 0     // true
```

The lack of transitivity is alarming. My advice is to never use the evil twins. Instead, always use `===` and `!==`. All of the comparisons just shown produce `false` with the `===` operator.

# with Statement

JavaScript has a with statement that was intended to provide a shorthand when accessing the properties of an object. Unfortunately, its results can sometimes be unpredictable, so it should be avoided.

The statement:

```
with (obj) {
    a = b;
}
```

does the same thing as:

```
if (obj.a === undefined) {
    a = obj.b === undefined ? b : obj.b;
} else {
    obj.a = obj.b === undefined ? b : obj.b;
}
```

So, it is the same as one of these statements:

```
a = b;
a = obj.b;
obj.a = b;
obj.a = obj.b;
```

It is not possible to tell from reading the program which of those statements you will get. It can vary from one running of the program to the next. It can even vary while the program is running. If you can't read a program and understand what it is going to do, it is impossible to have confidence that it will correctly do what you want.

Simply by being in the language, the with statement significantly slows down JavaScript processors because it frustrates the lexical binding of variable names. It was well intentioned, but the language would be better if it didn't have it.

# eval

The eval function passes a string to the JavaScript compiler and executes the result. It is the single most misused feature of JavaScript. It is most commonly used by people who have an incomplete understanding of the language. For example, if you know about the dot notation, but are ignorant of the subscript notation, you might write:

```
eval("myValue = myObject." + myKey + ";");
```

instead of:

```
myvalue = myObject[myKey];
```

The eval form is much harder to read. This form will be significantly slower because it needs to run the compiler just to execute a trivial assignment statement. It also frustrates JSLint (see Appendix C), so the tool's ability to detect problems is significantly reduced.

The eval function also compromises the security of your application because it grants too much authority to the eval'd text. And it compromises the performance of the language as a whole in the same way that the with statement does.

The Function constructor is another form of eval, and should similarly be avoided.

The browser provides setTimeout and setInterval functions that can take string arguments or function arguments. When given string arguments, setTimeout and setInterval act as eval. The string argument form also should be avoided.

## continue Statement

The continue statement jumps to the top of the loop. I have never seen a piece of code that was not improved by refactoring it to remove the continue statement.

## switch Fall Through

The switch statement was modeled after the FORTRAN IV computed go to statement. Each case falls through into the next case unless you explicitly disrupt the flow.

Someone wrote to me once suggesting that JSLint should give a warning when a case falls through into another case. He pointed out that this is a very common source of errors, and it is a difficult error to see in the code. I answered that that was all true, but that the benefit of compactness obtained by falling through more than compensated for the chance of error.

The next day, he reported that there was an error in JSLint. It was misidentifying an error. I investigated, and it turned out that I had a case that was falling through. In that moment, I achieved enlightenment. I no longer use intentional fall throughs. That discipline makes it much easier to find the unintentional fall throughs.

The worst features of a language aren't the features that are obviously dangerous or useless. Those are easily avoided. The worst features are the attractive nuisances, the features that are both useful and dangerous.

## Block-less Statements

An if or while or do or for statement can take a block or a single statement. The single statement form is another attractive nuisance. It offers the advantage of saving two characters, a dubious advantage. It obscures the program's structure so that subsequent manipulators of the code can easily insert bugs. For example:

```
if (ok)
    t = true;
```

can become:

```
if (ok)
    t = true;
    advance( );
```

which looks like:

```
if (ok) {
    t = true;
    advance( );
}
```

but which actually means:

```
if (ok) {
    t = true;
}
advance( );
```

Programs that appear to do one thing but actually do another are much harder to get right. A disciplined and consistent use of blocks makes it easier to get it right.

# ++ --

The increment and decrement operators make it possible to write in an extremely terse style. In languages such as C, they made it possible to write one-liners that could do string copies:

```
for (p = src, q = dest; !*p; p++, q++) *q = *p;
```

They also encourage a programming style that, as it turns out, is reckless. Most of the buffer overrun bugs that created terrible security vulnerabilities were due to code like this.

In my own practice, I observed that when I used ++ and --, my code tended to be too tight, too tricky, too cryptic. So, as a matter of discipline, I don't use them any more. I think that as a result, my coding style has become cleaner.

# Bitwise Operators

JavaScript has the same set of bitwise operators as Java:

```
&     and
|     or
^     xor
~     not
>>    signed right shift
>>>   unsigned right shift
<<    left shift
```

In Java, the bitwise operators work with integers. JavaScript doesn't have integers. It only has double precision floating-point numbers. So, the bitwise operators convert their number operands into integers, do their business, and then convert them back. In most languages, these operators are very close to the hardware and very fast. In JavaScript, they are very far from the hardware and very slow. JavaScript is rarely used for doing bit manipulation.

As a result, in JavaScript programs, it is more likely that & is a mistyped && operator. The presence of the bitwise operators reduces some of the language's redundancy, making it easier for bugs to hide.

# The function Statement Versus the function Expression

JavaScript has a function statement as well as a function expression. This is confusing because they can look exactly the same. A function statement is shorthand for a var statement with a function value.

The statement:

```
function foo( ) {}
```

means about the same thing as:

```
var foo = function foo( ) {};
```

Throughout this book, I have been using the second form because it makes it clear that foo is a variable containing a function value. To use the language well, it is important to understand that functions are values.

function statements are subject to *hoisting*. This means that regardless of where a function is placed, it is moved to the top of the scope in which it is defined. This relaxes the requirement that functions should be declared before used, which I think leads to sloppiness. It also prohibits the use of function statements in if statements. It turns out that most browsers allow function statements in if statements, but they vary in how that should be interpreted. That creates portability problems.

The first thing in a statement cannot be a function expression because the official grammar assumes that a statement that starts with the word function is a function statement. The workaround is to wrap the whole invocation in parentheses:

```
(function ( ) {
    var hidden_variable;

    // This function can have some impact on
    // the environment, but introduces no new
    // global variables.
}( ));
```

# Typed Wrappers

JavaScript has a set of typed wrappers. For example:

```
new Boolean(false)
```

produces an object that has a valueOf method that returns the wrapped value. This turns out to be completely unnecessary and occasionally confusing. Don't use new Boolean or new Number or new String.

Also avoid new Object and new Array. Use {} and [] instead.

## new

JavaScript's new operator creates a new object that inherits from the operand's prototype member, and then calls the operand, binding the new object to this. This gives the operand (which had better be a constructor function) a chance to customize the new object before it is returned to the requestor.

If you forget to use the new operator, you instead get an ordinary function call, and this is bound to the global object instead of to a new object. That means that your function will be clobbering global variables when it attempts to initialize the new members. That is a very bad thing. There is no compile-time warning. There is no runtime warning.

By convention, functions that are intended to be used with new should be given names with initial capital letters, and names with initial capital letters should be used only with constructor functions that take the new prefix. This convention gives us a visual cue that can help spot expensive mistakes that the language itself is keen to overlook.

An even better coping strategy is to not use new at all.

## void

In many languages, void is a type that has no values. In JavaScript, void is an operator that takes an operand and returns undefined. This is not useful, and it is very confusing. Avoid void.

# JSLint

*What error drives our eyes and ears amiss?*
—William Shakespeare, *The Comedy of Errors*

When C was a young programming language, there were several common programming errors that were not caught by the primitive compilers, so an accessory program called lint was developed that would scan a source file, looking for problems.

As C matured, the definition of the language was strengthened to eliminate some insecurities, and compilers got better at issuing warnings. lint is no longer needed.

JavaScript is a young-for-its-age language. It was originally intended to do small tasks in web pages, tasks for which Java was too heavy and clumsy. But JavaScript is a very capable language, and it is now being used in larger projects. Many of the features that were intended to make the language easy to use are troublesome for larger projects. A lint for JavaScript is needed: JSLint, a JavaScript syntax checker and verifier.

JSLint is a code quality tool for JavaScript. It takes a source text and scans it. If it finds a problem, it returns a message describing the problem and an approximate location within the source. The problem is not necessarily a syntax error, although it often is. JSLint looks at some style conventions as well as structural problems. It does not prove that your program is correct. It just provides another set of eyes to help spot problems.

JSLint defines a professional subset of JavaScript, a stricter language than that defined by the third edition of the *ECMAScript Language Specification*. The subset is closely related to the style recommendations from Chapter 9.

JavaScript is a sloppy language, but inside it there is an elegant, better language. JSLint helps you to program in that better language and to avoid most of the slop.

JSLint can be found at *http://www.JSLint.com/*.

# Undefined Variables and Functions

JavaScript's biggest problem is its dependence on global variables, particularly implied global variables. If a variable is not explicitly declared (usually with the var statement), then JavaScript assumes that the variable was global. This can mask misspelled names and other problems.

JSLint expects that all variables and functions will be declared before they are used or invoked. This allows it to detect implied global variables. It is also good practice because it makes programs easier to read.

Sometimes a file is dependent on global variables and functions that are defined elsewhere. You can identify these to JSLint by including a comment in your file that lists the global functions and objects that your program depends on, but that are not defined in your program or script file.

A global declaration comment can be used to list all of the names that you are intentionally using as global variables. JSLint can use this information to identify misspellings and forgotten var declarations. A global declaration can look like this:

```
/*global getElementByAttribute, breakCycles, hanoi */
```

A global declaration starts with /*global. Notice that there is no space before the g. You can have as many /*global comments as you like. They must appear before the use of the variables they specify.

Some globals can be predefined for you (see the later section "Options"). Select the "Assume a browser" (browser) option to predefine the standard global properties that are supplied by web browsers, such as window and document and alert. Select the "Assume Rhino" (rhino) option to predefine the global properties provided by the Rhino environment. Select the "Assume a Yahoo Widget" (widget) option to predefine the global properties provided by the Yahoo! Widgets environment.

# Members

Since JavaScript is a loosely typed dynamic-object language, it is not possible to determine at compile time if property names are spelled correctly. JSLint provides some assistance with this.

At the bottom of its report, JSLint displays a /*members*/ comment. It contains all of the names and string literals that were used with dot notation, subscript notation, and object literals to name the members of objects. You can look through the list for misspellings. Member names that were used only once are shown in italics. This is to make misspellings easier to spot.

You can copy the /*members*/ comment into your script file. JSLint will check the spelling of all property names against the list. That way, you can have JSLint look for misspellings for you:

```
/*members doTell, iDoDeclare, mercySakes,
    myGoodness, ohGoOn, wellShutMyMouth */
```

# Options

The implementation of JSLint accepts an option object that allows you to determine the subset of JavaScript that is acceptable to you. It is also possible to set those options within the source of a script.

An option specification can look like this:

```
/*jslint nomen: true, evil: false */
```

An option specification starts with /*jslint. Notice that there is no space before the j. The specification contains a sequence of name/value pairs, where the names are JSLint options and the values are true or false. An option specification takes precedence over the option object. All of the options default to false. Table C-1 lists the options available in using JSLint.

*Table C-1. JSLint options*

| Option | Meaning |
| --- | --- |
| adsafe | true if ADsafe.org rules should be enforced |
| bitwise | true if bitwise operators should not be allowed |
| browser | true if the standard browser globals should be predefined |
| cap | true if uppercase HTML should be allowed |
| debug | true if debugger statements should be allowed |
| eqeqeq | true if === should be required |
| evil | true if eval should be allowed |
| forin | true if unfiltered for in statements should be allowed |
| fragment | true if HTML fragments should be allowed |
| laxbreak | true if statement breaks should not be checked |
| nomen | true if names should be checked |
| on | true if HTML event handlers should be allowed |
| passfail | true if the scan should stop on first error |
| plusplus | true if ++ and -- should not be allowed |
| rhino | true if the Rhino environment globals should be predefined |
| undef | true if undefined global variables are errors |
| white | true if strict whitespace rules apply |
| widget | true if the Yahoo! Widgets globals should be predefined |

**JSLint comment**

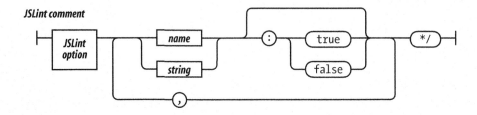

**option**

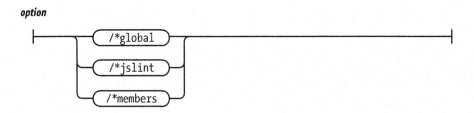

# Semicolon

JavaScript uses a C-like syntax, which requires the use of semicolons to delimit statements. JavaScript attempts to make semicolons optional with a semicolon insertion mechanism. This is dangerous.

Like C, JavaScript has ++ and -- and ( operators, which can be prefixes or suffixes. The disambiguation is done by the semicolon.

In JavaScript, a linefeed can be whitespace, or it can act as a semicolon. This replaces one ambiguity with another.

JSLint expects that every statement be followed by ; except for for, function, if, switch, try, and while. JSLint does not expect to see unnecessary semicolons or the empty statement.

# Line Breaking

As a further defense against the masking of errors by the semicolon insertion mechanism, JSLint expects long statements to be broken only after one of these punctuation characters or operators:

```
, ; : { } ( [ = < > ? ! + - * / % ~ ^ | &
== != <= >= += -= *= /= %= ^= |= &= << >> || &&
=== !== <<= >>= >>> >>>=
```

JSLint does not expect to see a long statement broken after an identifier, a string, a number, a closer, or a suffix operator:

```
) ] . ++ --
```

JSLint allows you to turn on the "Tolerate sloppy line breaking" (laxbreak) option.

Semicolon insertion can mask copy/paste errors. If you always break lines after operators, then JSLint can do a better job of finding those errors.

# Comma

The comma operator can lead to excessively tricky expressions. It can also mask some programming errors.

JSLint expects to see the comma used as a separator, but not as an operator (except in the initialization and incrementation parts of the for statement). It does not expect to see elided elements in array literals. Extra commas should not be used. A comma should not appear after the last element of an array literal or object literal because it can be misinterpreted by some browsers.

# Required Blocks

JSLint expects that if and for statements will be made with blocks—that is, with statements enclosed in braces ({}).

JavaScript allows an if to be written like this:

```
if (condition)
    statement;
```

That form is known to contribute to mistakes in projects where many programmers are working on the same code. That is why JSLint expects the use of a block:

```
if (condition) {
    statements;
}
```

Experience shows that this form is more resilient.

# Forbidden Blocks

In many languages, a block introduces a scope. Variables introduced in a block are not visible outside of the block.

In JavaScript, blocks do not introduce a scope. There is only function-scope. A variable introduced anywhere in a function is visible everywhere in the function. JavaScript's blocks confuse experienced programmers and lead to errors because the familiar syntax makes a false promise.

JSLint expects blocks with function, if, switch, while, for, do, and try statements and nowhere else. An exception is made for an unblocked if statement on an else or for in.

# Expression Statements

An expression statement is expected to be an assignment, a function/method call, or delete. All other expression statements are considered errors.

# for in Statement

The for in statement allows for looping through the names of all of the properties of an object. Unfortunately, it also loops through all of the members that were inherited through the prototype chain. This has the bad side effect of serving up method functions when the interest is in the data members.

The body of every for in statement should be wrapped in an if statement that does filtering. if can select for a particular type or range of values, it can exclude functions, or it can exclude properties from the prototype. For example:

```
for (name in object) {
    if (object.hasOwnProperty(name)) {
        ....
    }
}
```

# switch Statement

A common error in switch statements is to forget to place a break statement after each case, resulting in unintended fall-through. JSLint expects that the statement before the next case or default is one of these: break, return, or throw.

# var Statement

JavaScript allows var definitions to occur anywhere within a function. JSLint is stricter.

JSLint expects that:

- A var will be declared only once, and that it will be declared before it is used.
- A function will be declared before it is used.
- Parameters will not also be declared as vars.

JSLint does not expect:

- The arguments array to be declared as a var.
- That a variable will be declared in a block. This is because JavaScript blocks do not have block scope. This can have unexpected consequences, so define all variables at the top of the function body.

# with Statement

The with statement was intended to provide a shorthand in accessing members in deeply nested objects. Unfortunately, it behaves very badly when setting new members. Never use the with statement. Use a var instead.

JSLint does not expect to see a with statement.

# =

JSLint does not expect to see an assignment statement in the condition part of an if or while statement. This is because it is more likely that:

```
if (a = b) {
    ...
}
```

was intended to be:

```
if (a == b) {
    ...
}
```

If you really intend an assignment, wrap it in another set of parentheses:

```
if ((a = b)) {
    ...
}
```

# == and !=

The == and != operators do type coercion before comparing. This is bad because it causes ' \f\r \n\t ' == 0 to be true. This can mask type errors.

When comparing to any of the following values, always use the === or !== operators, which do not do type coercion:

```
0 '' undefined null false true
```

If you want the type coercion, then use the short form. Instead of:

```
(foo != 0)
```

just say:

```
(foo)
```

And instead of:

```
(foo == 0)
```

say:

```
(!foo)
```

Use of the `===` and `!==` operators is always preferred. There is a "Disallow `==` and `!=`" (eqeqeq) option, which requires the use of `===` and `!==` in all cases.

# Labels

JavaScript allows any statement to have a label, and labels have a separate namespace. JSLint is stricter.

JSLint expects labels only on statements that interact with break: `switch`, `while`, `do`, and `for`. JSLint expects that labels will be distinct from variables and parameters.

# Unreachable Code

JSLint expects that a `return`, `break`, `continue`, or `throw` statement will be followed by a } or case or `default`.

# Confusing Pluses and Minuses

JSLint expects that + will not be followed by + or ++, and that - will not be followed by - or --. A misplaced space can turn + + into ++, an error that is difficult to see. Use parentheses to avoid confusion.

# ++ and --

The ++ (increment) and -- (decrement) operators have been known to contribute to bad code by encouraging excessive trickiness. They are second only to faulty architecture in enabling viruses and other security menaces. The JSLint option plusplus prohibits the use of these operators.

# Bitwise Operators

JavaScript does not have an integer type, but it does have bitwise operators. The bitwise operators convert their operands from floating-point to integers and back, so they are not nearly as efficient as they are in C or other languages. They are rarely useful in browser applications. The similarity to the logical operators can mask some programming errors. The bitwise option prohibits the use of these operators.

# eval Is Evil

The eval function and its relatives (`Function`, `setTimeout`, and `setInterval`) provide access to the JavaScript compiler. This is sometimes useful, but in most cases it indicates the presence of extremely bad coding. The eval function is the most misused feature of JavaScript.

# void

In most C-like languages, void is a type. In JavaScript, void is a prefix operator that always returns undefined. JSLint does not expect to see void because it is confusing and not very useful.

# Regular Expressions

Regular expressions are written in a terse and cryptic notation. JSLint looks for problems that may cause portability problems. It also attempts to resolve visual ambiguities by recommending explicit escapement.

JavaScript's syntax for regular expression literals overloads the / character. To avoid ambiguity, JSLint expects that the character preceding a regular expression literal is a ( or = or : or , character.

# Constructors and new

Constructors are functions that are designed to be used with the new prefix. The new prefix creates a new object based on the function's prototype, and binds that object to the function's implied this parameter. If you neglect to use the new prefix, no new object will be made, and this will be bound to the global object. This is a serious mistake.

JSLint enforces the convention that constructor functions be given names with initial uppercase letters. JSLint does not expect to see a function invocation with an initial uppercase name unless it has the new prefix. JSLint does not expect to see the new prefix used with functions whose names do not start with initial uppercase.

JSLint does not expect to see the wrapper forms new Number, new String, or new Boolean.

JSLint does not expect to see new Object (use {} instead).

JSLint does not expect to see new Array (use [ ] instead).

# Not Looked For

JSLint does not do flow analysis to determine that variables are assigned values before they are used. This is because variables are given a value (undefined) that is a reasonable default for many applications.

JSLint does not do any kind of global analysis. It does not attempt to determine that functions used with new are really constructors (except by enforcing capitalization conventions), or that method names are spelled correctly.

# HTML

JSLint is able to handle HTML text. It can inspect the JavaScript content contained within <script>...</script> tags and event handlers. It also inspects the HTML content, looking for problems that are known to interfere with JavaScript:

- All tag names must be in lowercase.
- All tags that can take a close tag (such as </p>) must have a close tag.
- All tags are correctly nested.
- The entity &lt; must be used for literal <.

JSLint is less anal than the sycophantic conformity demanded by XHTML, but more strict than the popular browsers.

JSLint also checks for the occurrence of </ in string literals. You should always write <\/ instead. The extra backslash is ignored by the JavaScript compiler, but not by the HTML parser. Tricks like this should not be necessary, and yet they are.

There is an option that allows use of uppercase tag names. There is also an option that allows the use of inline HTML event handlers.

# JSON

JSLint can also check that JSON data structures are well formed. If the first character JSLint sees is { or [, then it strictly enforces the JSON rules. See Appendix E.

# Report

If JSLint is able to complete its scan, it generates a function report. It lists the following for each function:

- The line number on which it starts.
- Its name. In the case of anonymous functions, JSLint will "guess" the name.
- The parameters.
- Closure: the variables and parameters that are declared in the function that are used by its inner functions.
- Variables: the variables declared in the function that are used only by the function.
- Unused: the variables that are declared in the function that are not used. This may be an indication of an error.
- Outer: variables used by this function that are declared in another function.
- Global: global variables that are used by this function.
- Label: statement labels that are used by this function.

The report will also include a list of all of the member names that were used.

# Syntax Diagrams

*Thou map of woe, that thus dost talk in signs!*
—William Shakespeare, *The Tragedy of Titus Andronicus*

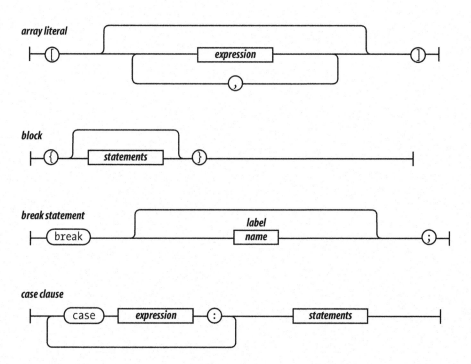

**disruptive statement**

**do statement**

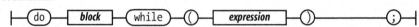

**escaped character**

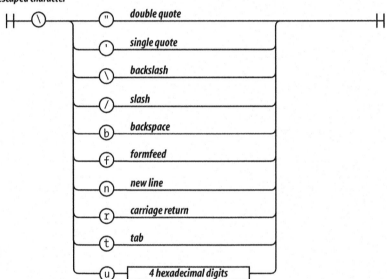

**exponent**

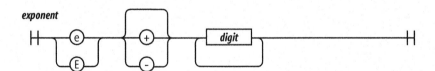

*expression*

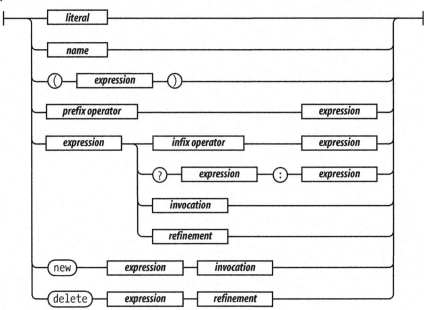

*expression statement*

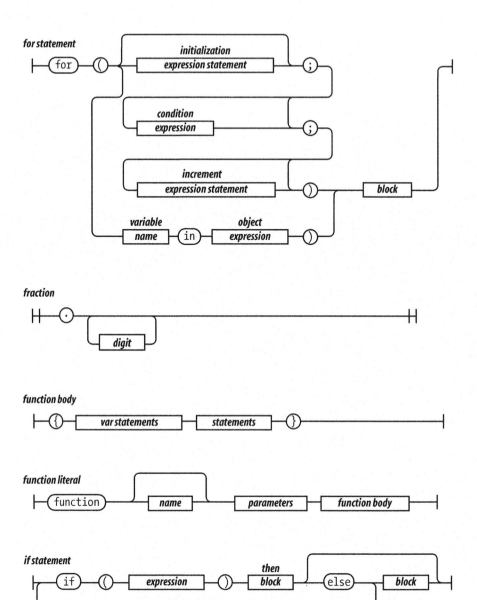

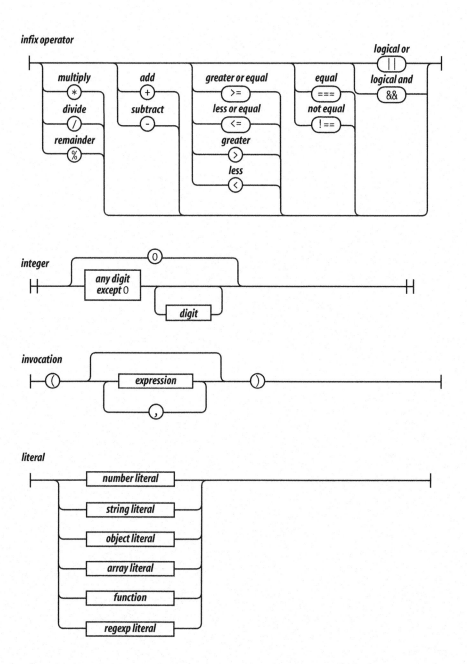

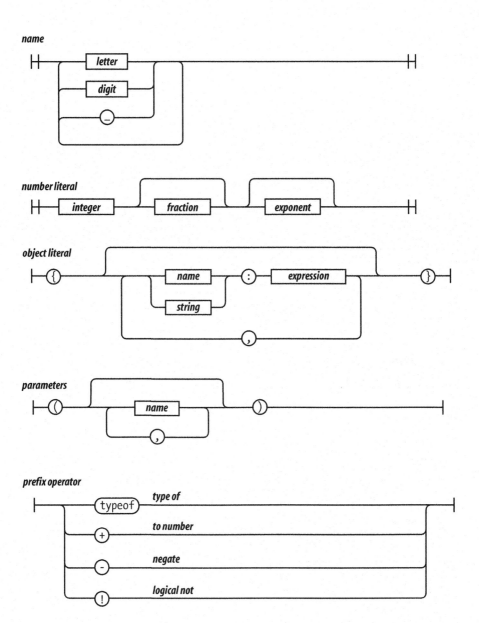

*refinement*

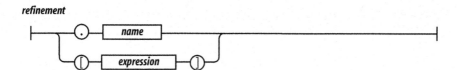

*regexp choice*

*regexp class*

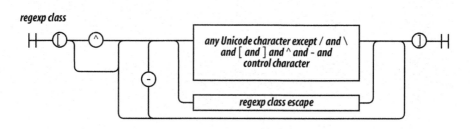

*regexp class escape*

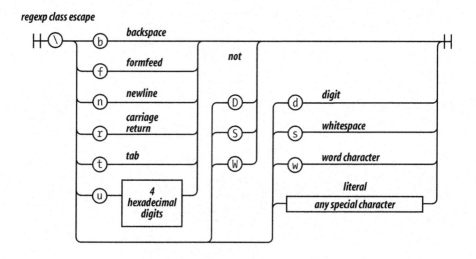

*regexp escape*

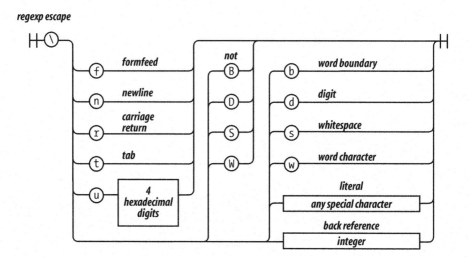

*regexp factor*

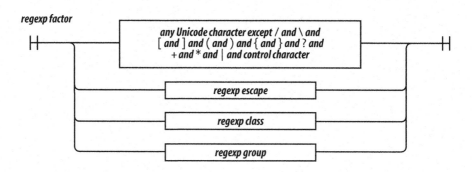

*regexp group*

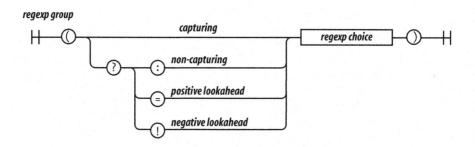

*regexp literal*

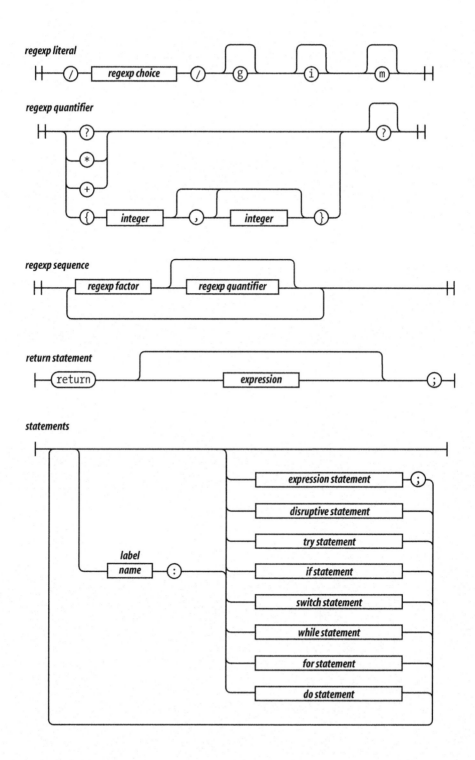

*regexp quantifier*

*regexp sequence*

*return statement*

*statements*

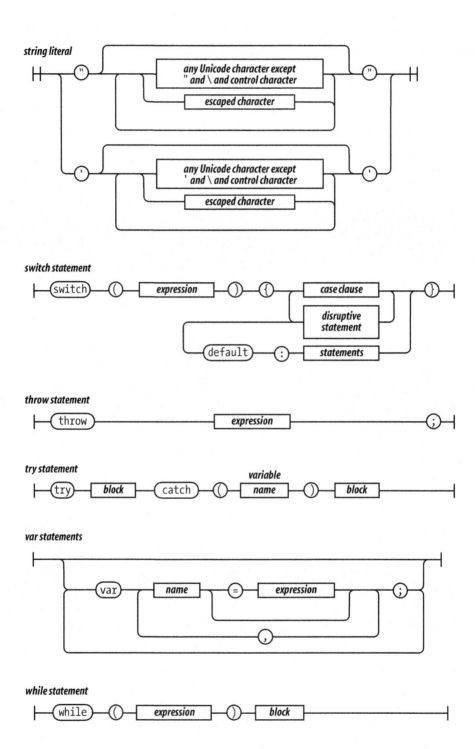

*string literal*

*switch statement*

*throw statement*

*try statement*

*var statements*

*while statement*

**whitespace**

# APPENDIX E

# JSON

*Farewell: the leisure and the fearful time*
*Cuts off the ceremonious vows of love*
*And ample interchange of sweet discourse,*
*Which so long sunder'd friends should dwell upon:*
*God give us leisure for these rites of love!*
*Once more, adieu: be valiant, and speed well!*
—William Shakespeare, *The Tragedy of Richard the Third*

JavaScript Object Notation (JSON) is a lightweight data interchange format. It is based on JavaScript's object literal notation, one of JavaScript's best parts. Even though it is a subset of JavaScript, it is language independent. It can be used to exchange data between programs written in all modern programming languages. It is a text format, so it is readable by humans and machines. It is easy to implement and easy to use. There is a lot of material about JSON at *http://www.JSON.org/*.

## JSON Syntax

JSON has six kinds of values: objects, arrays, strings, numbers, booleans (true and false), and the special value null. Whitespace (spaces, tabs, carriage returns, and newline characters) may be inserted before or after any value. This can make JSON texts easier for humans to read. Whitespace may be omitted to reduce transmission or storage costs.

A JSON object is an unordered container of name/value pairs. A name can be any string. A value can be any JSON value, including arrays and objects. JSON objects can be nested to any depth, but generally it is most effective to keep them relatively flat. Most languages have a feature that maps easily to JSON objects, such as an object, struct, record, dictionary, hash table, property list, or associative array.

The JSON array is an ordered sequence of values. A value can be any JSON value, including arrays and objects. Most languages have a feature that maps easily onto JSON arrays, such as an array, vector, list, or sequence.

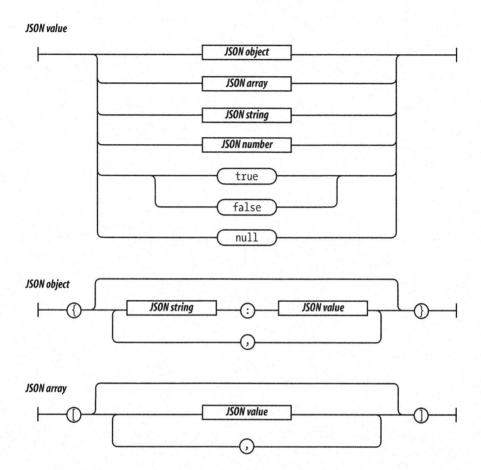

A JSON string is wrapped in double quotes. The \ character is used for escapement. JSON allows the / character to be escaped so that JSON can be embedded in HTML `<script>` tags. HTML does not allow the sequence `</` except to start the `</script>` tag. JSON allows `<\/`, which produces the same result but does not confuse HTML.

JSON numbers are like JavaScript numbers. A leading zero is not allowed on integers because some languages use that to indicate the octal. That kind of radix confusion is not desirable in a data interchange format. A number can be an integer, real, or scientific.

That's it. That is all of JSON. JSON's design goals were to be minimal, portable, textual, and a subset of JavaScript. The less we need to agree on in order to interoperate, the more easily we can interoperate.

**JSON string**

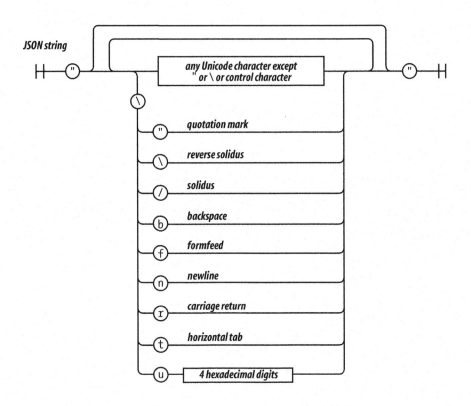

**JSON number**

```
[
    {
        "first": "Jerome",
        "middle": "Lester",
        "last": "Howard",
        "nick-name": "Curly",
        "born": 1903,
        "died": 1952,
        "quote": "nyuk-nyuk-nyuk!"
```

```
    },
    {
        "first": "Harry",
        "middle": "Moses",
        "last": "Howard",
        "nick-name": "Moe",
        "born": 1897,
        "died": 1975,
        "quote": "Why, you!"
    },
    {
        "first": "Louis",
        "last": "Feinberg",
        "nick-name": "Larry",
        "born": 1902,
        "died": 1975,
        "quote": "I'm sorry. Moe, it was an accident!"
    }
]
```

# Using JSON Securely

JSON is particularly easy to use in web applications because JSON is JavaScript. A JSON text can be turned into a useful data structure with the eval function:

```
var myData = eval('(' + myJSONText + ')');
```

(The concatenation of the parentheses around the JSON text is a workaround for an ambiguity in JavaScript's grammar.)

The eval function has horrendous security problems, however. Is it safe to use eval to parse a JSON text? Currently, the best technique for obtaining data from a server in a web browser is through XMLHttpRequest. XMLHttpRequest can obtain data only from the same server that produced the HTML. evaling text from that server is no less secure than the original HTML. But, that assumes the server is malicious. What if the server is simply incompetent?

An incompetent server might not do the JSON encoding correctly. If it builds JSON texts by slapping together some strings rather than using a proper JSON encoder, then it could unintentionally send dangerous material. If it acts as a proxy and simply passes JSON text through without determining whether it is well formed, then it could send dangerous material again.

The danger can be avoided by using the JSON.parse method instead of eval (see *http://www.JSON.org/json2.js*). JSON.parse will throw an exception if the text contains anything dangerous. It is recommended that you always use JSON.parse instead of eval to defend against server incompetence. It is also good practice for the day when the browser provides safe data access to other servers.

There is another danger in the interaction between external data and innerHTML. A common Ajax pattern is for the server to send an HTML text fragment that gets assigned to the innerHTML property of an HTML element. This is a very bad practice. If the HTML text contains a <script> tag or its equivalent, then an evil script will run. This again could be due to server incompetence.

What specifically is the danger? If an evil script gets to run on your page, it gets access to all of the state and capabilities of the page. It can interact with your server, and your server will not be able to distinguish the evil requests from legitimate requests. The evil script has access to the global object, which gives it access to all of the data in the application except for variables hidden in closures. It has access to the document object, which gives it access to everything that the user sees. It also gives the evil script the capability to dialog with the user. The browser's location bar and all of the anti-phishing chrome will tell the user that the dialog should be trusted. The document object also gives the evil script access to the network, allowing it to load more evil scripts, or to probe for sites within your firewall, or to send the secrets it has learned to any server in the world.

This danger is a direct consequence of JavaScript's global object, which is far and away the worst part of JavaScript's many bad parts. These dangers are not caused by Ajax or JSON or XMLHttpRequest or Web 2.0 (whatever that is). These dangers have been in the browser since the introduction of JavaScript, and will remain until JavaScript is replaced or repaired. Be careful.

# A JSON Parser

This is an implementation of a JSON parser in JavaScript:

```
var json_parse = function () {

// This is a function that can parse a JSON text, producing a JavaScript
// data structure. It is a simple, recursive descent parser.

// We are defining the function inside of another function to avoid creating
// global variables.

    var at,     // The index of the current character
        ch,     // The current character
        escapee = {
            '"':  '"',
            '\\': '\\',
            '/':  '/',
            b:    'b',
            f:    '\f',
            n:    '\n',
            r:    '\r',
            t:    '\t'
        },
```

```
        text,

        error = function (m) {
```

// Call error when something is wrong.

```
            throw {
                name:    'SyntaxError',
                message: m,
                at:      at,
                text:    text
            };
        },

        next = function (c) {
```

// If a c parameter is provided, verify that it matches the current character.

```
            if (c && c !== ch) {
                error("Expected '" + c + "' instead of '" + ch + "'");
            }
```

// Get the next character. When there are no more characters,
// return the empty string.

```
            ch = text.charAt(at);
            at += 1;
            return ch;
        },

        number = function () {
```

// Parse a number value.

```
            var number,
                string = '';

            if (ch === '-') {
                string = '-';
                next('-');
            }
            while (ch >= '0' && ch <= '9') {
                string += ch;
                next();
            }
            if (ch === '.') {
                string += '.';
                while (next() && ch >= '0' && ch <= '9') {
                    string += ch;
                }
            }
            if (ch === 'e' || ch === 'E') {
                string += ch;
                next();
```

```
            if (ch === '-' || ch === '+') {
                string += ch;
                next();
            }
            while (ch >= '0' && ch <= '9') {
                string += ch;
                next();
            }
        }
        number = +string;
        if (isNaN(number)) {
            error("Bad number");
        } else {
            return number;
        }
    },

    string = function () {

// Parse a string value.

        var hex,
            i,
            string = '',
            uffff;

// When parsing for string values, we must look for " and \ characters.

        if (ch === '"') {
            while (next()) {
                if (ch === '"') {
                    next();
                    return string;
                } else if (ch === '\\') {
                    next();
                    if (ch === 'u') {
                        uffff = 0;
                        for (i = 0; i < 4; i += 1) {
                            hex = parseInt(next(), 16);
                            if (!isFinite(hex)) {
                                break;
                            }
                            uffff = uffff * 16 + hex;
                        }
                        string += String.fromCharCode(uffff);
                    } else if (typeof escapee[ch] === 'string') {
                        string += escapee[ch];
                    } else {
                        break;
                    }
                } else {
                    string += ch;
                }
            }
        }
```

```
            }
            error("Bad string");
        },

        white = function () {

// Skip whitespace.

            while (ch && ch <= ' ') {
                next();
            }
        },

        word = function () {

// true, false, or null.

            switch (ch) {
            case 't':
                next('t');
                next('r');
                next('u');
                next('e');
                return true;
            case 'f':
                next('f');
                next('a');
                next('l');
                next('s');
                next('e');
                return false;
            case 'n':
                next('n');
                next('u');
                next('l');
                next('l');
                return null;
            }
            error("Unexpected '" + ch + "'");
        },

        value,  // Place holder for the value function.

        array = function () {

// Parse an array value.

            var array = [];

            if (ch === '[') {
                next('[');
                white();
                if (ch === ']') {
                    next(']');
                    return array;   // empty array
```

```
                }
                while (ch) {
                    array.push(value());
                    white();
                    if (ch === ']') {
                        next(']');
                        return array;
                    }
                    next(',');
                    white();
                }
            }
            error("Bad array");
        },

        object = function () {

// Parse an object value.

            var key,
                object = {};

            if (ch === '{') {
                next('{');
                white();
                if (ch === '}') {
                    next('}');
                    return object;    // empty object
                }
                while (ch) {
                    key = string();
                    white();
                    next(':');
                    object[key] = value();
                    white();
                    if (ch === '}') {
                        next('}');
                        return object;
                    }
                    next(',');
                    white();
                }
            }
            error("Bad object");
        };

    value = function () {

// Parse a JSON value. It could be an object, an array, a string, a number,
// or a word.

        white();
        switch (ch) {
        case '{':
            return object();
```

```
            case '[':
                return array();
            case '"':
                return string();
            case '-':
                return number();
            default:
                return ch >= '0' && ch <= '9' ? number() : word();
            }
        };

// Return the json_parse function. It will have access to all of the above
// functions and variables.

        return function (source, reviver) {
            var result;

            text = source;
            at = 0;
            ch = ' ';
            result = value();
            white();
            if (ch) {
                error("Syntax error");
            }

// If there is a reviver function, we recursively walk the new structure,
// passing each name/value pair to the reviver function for possible
// transformation, starting with a temporary boot object that holds the result
// in an empty key. If there is not a reviver function, we simply return the
// result.

            return typeof reviver === 'function' ?
                function walk(holder, key) {
                    var k, v, value = holder[key];
                    if (value && typeof value === 'object') {
                        for (k in value) {
                            if (Object.hasOwnProperty.call(value, k)) {
                                v = walk(value, k);
                                if (v !== undefined) {
                                    value[k] = v;
                                } else {
                                    delete value[k];
                                }
                            }
                        }
                    }
                    return reviver.call(holder, key, value);
                }({'': result}, '') : result;

        };
    }();
```

# Index

We'd like to hear your suggestions for improving our indexes. Send email to *index@oreilly.com*.

## About the Author

**Douglas Crockford** is a senior JavaScript architect at Yahoo! who is well known for discovering and popularizing the JSON (JavaScript Object Notation) format. He is the world's foremost living authority on JavaScript. He speaks regularly at conferences about advanced web technology, and he also serves on the ECMAScript committee.

## Colophon

The animal on the cover of *JavaScript: The Good Parts* is a Plain Tiger butterfly (*Danaus chrysippus*). Outside of Asia, the insect is also known as the African Monarch. It is a medium-size butterfly characterized by bright orange wings with six black spots and alternating black-and-white stripes.

Its striking looks have been noted for millennia by scientists and artists. The writer Vladimir Nabokov—who was also a noted lepidopterist—had admiring words for the butterfly in an otherwise scathing *New York Times* book review of Alice Ford's *Audubon's Butterflies, Moths, and Other Studies* (The Studio Publications). In the book, Ford labels drawings made previous to and during Audubon's time in the 19th century as "scientifi-cally [*sic*] unsophisticated."

In response to Ford, Nabokov writes, "The unsophistication is all her own. She might have looked up John Abbot's prodigious representations of North American lepidoptera, 1797, or the splendid plates of 18th- and early-19th-century German lepidopterists. She might have traveled back some 33 centuries to the times of Tuthmosis IV or Amenophis III and, instead of the obvious scarab, found there frescoes with a marvelous Egyptian butterfly (subtly combining the pattern of our Painted Lady and the body of an African ally of the Monarch)."

While the Plain Tiger's beauty is part of its charm, its looks can also be deadly. During its larval stages, the butterfly ingests alkaloids that are poisonous to birds—its main predator—which are often attracted to the insect's markings. After ingesting the Plain Tiger, a bird will vomit repeatedly—occasionally fatally. If the bird lives, it will let other birds know to avoid the insect, which can also be recognized by its leisurely, meandering pattern of flying low to the earth.

The cover image is from *Dover's Animals*. The cover font is Adobe ITC Garamond. The text font is Linotype Birka; the heading font is Adobe Myriad Condensed; and the code font is LucasFont's TheSans Mono Condensed.

CPSIA information can be obtained at www.ICGtesting.com
Printed in the USA
BVOW09s1128050516

R7006100001B/R70061PG445947BVX1B/1/P